The Passion of the Christ

✕ Controversies

Series editors: Stevie Simkin and Julian Petley

Controversies is a series comprising individual studies of controversial films from the late 1960s to the present day, encompassing classic, contemporary Hollywood, cult and world cinema. Each volume provides an in-depth study analysing the various stages of each film's production, distribution, classification and reception, assessing both its impact at the time of its release and its subsequent legacy.

Also published

Stevie Simkin, *Straw Dogs*

Peter Krämer, *A Clockwork Orange*

Shaun Kimber, *Henry: Portrait of a Serial Killer*

Forthcoming

Lucy Burke, *The Idiots*

Gabrielle Murray, *Bad Boy Bubby*

Jude Davies, *Falling Down*

Julian Petley, *Crash*

Stevie Simkin, *Basic Instinct*

'The *Controversies* series is a valuable contribution to the ongoing debate about what limits – if any – should be placed on cinema when it comes to the depiction and discussion of extreme subject matter. Sober, balanced and insightful where much debate on these matters has been hysterical, one-sided and unhelpful, these books should help us get a perspective on some of the thorniest films in the history of cinema.'
Kim Newman, novelist, critic and broadcaster

The Passion of the Christ

Neal King

First published 2011 by
PALGRAVE MACMILLAN

Palgrave Macmillan in the UK is an imprint of Macmillan Publishers
Limited, registered in England, company number 785998, of Houndmills,
Basingstoke, Hampshire RG21 6XS.

Palgrave Macmillan in the US is a division of St Martin's Press LLC, 175
Fifth Avenue, New York, NY 10010.

Palgrave Macmillan is the global academic imprint of the above companies
and has companies and representatives throughout the world.

Palgrave® and Macmillan® are registered trademarks in the United States,
the United Kingdom, Europe and other countries.

ISBN-13: 978–0–230–29434–9

This book is printed on paper suitable for recycling and made from fully
managed and sustained forest sources. Logging, pulping and
manufacturing processes are expected to conform to the environmental
regulations of the country of origin.

A catalogue record for this book is available from the British Library.

A catalog record for this book is available from the Library of Congress.

10   9   8   7   6   5   4   3   2   1
20   19   18   17   16   15   14   13   12   11

Printed in China

Contents

Part 1: Production and Marketing

Part 2: Rating and Censorship

Part 3: Reception

Part 4: Plotting

Part 5: Key Scene Analysis

Part 6: Legacy

Appendices

Acknowledgments

I am indebted to Toni Calasanti, Elizabeth Struthers Malbon and Stephen Prince for fruitful discussion, and to Steve for going to the movie with me. I have also benefited from guidance by the series editors and a blind reviewer. Any problems remaining in these pages owe to my own sins and vice.

✕ Introduction

A scant several years have passed since the release of the American blockbuster
The Passion of the Christ (2004); but enough has occurred to give us short-term
perspective. We know how durable a theatrical blockbuster it is (not very), how
lasting its effect on screen violence will be (it raised the bar for graphic scenes
of torture in a few nations, but only long enough to slip through its initial
release), how its principal author feels about Jews (suspicious, at the least), and
whether he will ever do lunch in Hollywood again (Mel Gibson has since
suffered scandal and lost face in the industry). We do not know whether
anyone will want to see this movie in twenty years, but may suppose that it will,
at the very least, live in the film buff's memory as the centre of a notable storm.
In the year leading up to its release, *The Passion of the Christ* inspired one of the
largest controversies, and perhaps the most significant exception in the
regulation of film violence, since the late 1960s when such directors as Arthur
Penn and Sam Peckinpah sped the flow of movie blood.

I first saw *The Passion of the Christ* in March of 2004, at a suburban
theatre in the Bible Belt of Virginia, U.S.A. Older women sat alone and in
groups, weeping and chanting, 'Jesus, Jesus, Jesus. Lord, Lord, Lord.' Their
cries rose and fell with the intensity of the violence on screen, suggesting that,
for them, the brutality of this vision lay at the core of its meaning. Rather than
distract from the story, its spectacle was its point. And none of us had ever
seen such extensive, bloody torture in an R-rated film before. It struck me at
the time that an exception had been made.

I had also heard charges of anti-Semitism, and somewhere a denial by
Gibson, but had not pursued the matter in my reading on the film. As it
unspooled, I thought that Pilate compared awfully well to the thuggish

priests. And I knew that Cecil B. DeMille had been criticized for his own High Priest Caiaphas, played with cartoonish villainy by Rudolph Schildkraut in his 1927 silent *The King of Kings*. I remember thinking that Gibson seemed awfully anxious to replicate that scenario, and wondered why.

Most of my students had seen the film by the time I brought it up, in a course on movie violence that semester. Many had attended out of curiosity, to see what the fuss was about. Others went with Christian family and friends, or on their recommendations. The most immediate effect on classroom discussion was that students no longer protested claims about the meaning of the cross. I teach that blood sacrifice has been a focal point of both sectarian and civil religion (Marvin and Ingle, 1999); and for years I have mentioned to students that many regard the most immediate referent of the cross to be that of an instrument of execution. Some Christians in my classes had taken exception and insisted that violence was beside the point, that love, mercy and grace were the only matters symbolized. But no one says that any more. For good or for ill, this film has altered the meaning of the central symbol of Christendom. As the evangelical magazine *Christianity Today* put it, 'Unlike liberal Christians (both Catholic and Protestant) who deny the importance of the shedding of blood in the Atonement, Gibson grasps firmly the sacred symbol of blood and spatters the audience's sensibilities with it' (Neff, 2004, p. 35). Whatever it ought or will be decades hence, Christianity is a blood cult now, dwelling on the cross as a means of execution.

And so this Jesus movie did what no other had: became the object of ritual focus nationwide; compelled millions to watch graphic scenes of torture; and stirred American controversy over anti-Semitism and gospel fidelity on a level of the struggle over *The Last Temptation of Christ* – which, in 1988, had become the only object of prior censorship in the US in the second half of the twentieth century. This book places *The Passion of the Christ* in the broader contexts of a century of films about Christ and his passion, argument about portrayals of Jews, the regulation of film violence by boards around the world and the viewing habits of its principal supporters – conservative Protestants and Catholics in the US.

I first recount the events that led up to the blockbusting release, from the initial reports that piqued curiosity, to escalating conflict between rival groups. The increasingly hostile evangelicalism of the post-9/11 years in the US appears to have fanned flames of controversy under a film that might otherwise merely have smouldered. Scholars who questioned Gibson's intentions toward Jews walked into a marketing trap, in which their critique of Biblical literalism translated into enmity toward Christ and rallied evangelicals and conservative Catholics to support the release. The marketing blitz inspired pundits from the right to address Jews as a group with threats and disparagement seldom used in the US any more. Spokespeople on both sides resorted to exaggerations and imputations of evil that stemmed from the cascade of insults and misunderstandings, as well as from the divergence of the professional ties of clerics, filmmakers, pundits and scholars. By accusing each other of senseless malice, each side did its job.

That controversy seems also to have led several ratings boards to rethink their categories and lighten restriction of iconography and show-stopping torture. I argue that the massive support lent this film by evangelical groups put ratings boards in the awkward position of potentially *offending* watchdogs by being restrictive. Contrasting cases in the US and New Zealand allow us to infer the pressure under which ratings boards worked. In other cases, the religious status of the movie appears to have helped it gain wider release despite rules against depictions of prophets. Thus some nations have relaxed restrictions on the release not *despite* the controversy over anti-Semitism but *because* of it.

The release also appears to have prompted anti-media violence watchdog groups to devise a new category of bloodshed in cinema. Where they would usually condemn onscreen violence as conducive of vice and possibly crime, many evangelical critics came to regard depiction of the ravaging of Christ as redemptive. Their supportive criticism of the film contrasts sharply with scholarly and pop-critical rejection of it. That support served a larger mission to use entertainment to do holy work and to fight for control of the popular storytelling that Hollywood has usurped.

The rest of the book narrows its focus to the film itself, reviewing patterns in its storytelling and the stated intentions and techniques of its makers. The film is acted, shot, scored and edited in the fashion of most Hollywood features. And it maintains a stance toward its central character typical of the most successful gospel adaptations, by not plotting his dramatic arc but dwelling instead on the responses of onlookers. I suggest that this decision by the filmmakers, which alienated those who prefer to listen to Christ's teaching than to watch his suffering, helped it to garner a warm welcome from conservative Christians.

I next add my two cents to the debate over anti-Semitism with a close reading of the face-off between Roman and Judean authorities, and comments made by the filmmakers about it. It is difficult to conclude, from a study of this scene, that the storytelling is neutral toward the contestants. The scripting, acting, framing and editing oppose a thoughtful Roman governor and his sensitive wife to malicious Judeans. Drawing on contrasting accounts (gospel and anti-Semitic ruminations) and accompanied by contrasting explanations from Gibson's colleagues (Pilate as the bad guy vs Caiphas as the guiltiest one), and appearing in at least two versions in public release, the scene is a suitably complex focal point for one of the greatest controversies in contemporary Hollywood.

I conclude with a summary of this film's short legacy. It has made little news in the years since its debut, save for notice of its failure on rerelease, and of a drunken Gibson critiquing Jews in 2006. The scandals over the film and filmmaker, along with the assimilation of evangelical culture in the US, suggest that we are unlikely to see another such polarizing controversy soon. The release of *The Passion of the Christ* is likely to remain a remarkable anomaly, an evangelical blockbuster and vehicle for the expression of a subculture's waning authority, which vented racial hostility and led ratings boards and watchdog groups to bend rules on depictions of torture.

✕ A Personal and Procedural Note

I have no insider status within Hollywood to speak of, but approach this book as a scholar with ties to groups involved. First, I was raised Protestant in a family named for an actor who played such royalty as Herod in passion plays. My mother performed in one such Lenten play (Rev. Don A. Mueller's devotional *Eyes upon the Cross*) for decades, crewing while pregnant with me but otherwise on stage as Claudia or Magdalene. My family of origin maintains enthusiastic mainline and evangelical activity today.

Second, I married an alumna of Loyola Marymount University, a Jesuit school located not far from the Santa Monica offices of Gibson's Icon Productions. That university encompasses networks of enthusiastic and often conservative Catholics, such as archaeologist William Fulco, who transcribed the script and served as coach and theologian on the set. Its College of Fine Arts has trained many Hollywood personnel, such as Steve McEveety, who produced *The Passion of the Christ* for Icon.

Third, I am one of a large group of scholars who treat religion as an object of scientific study, which approach can contrast with orthodoxy (such scholars tend to be more liberal than evangelicals, for instance). I am also marginal to a smaller network that specializes in gospels and first-century Palestine. Though I have no special expertise and do not publish in the area, I have had the pleasure of working with one such researcher (see Malbon, 2000).

Finally, I have enjoyed, as a movie buff, Mel Gibson's performances in action movies for decades. I care little for his directorial work, infer nothing of his private life from his screen persona, and do not align with what I have read of his politics and temperament; but I have taken pleasure in his work before the camera – from Australian revenge flicks to his latest cop action (2010's *Edge of Darkness*, which I liked just fine).

This does not mean that I see all sides to everything, but it does mean that I keep company with diverse viewers, who sympathize with opposing parties and sides of the arguments. When I use terms *scholars, fans, conservative Catholics, Jews* and *evangelicals,* I write not of alien groups but of family and friends. When I review the evidence before me, I remain sceptical of self-serving publicity statements and cross-check veracity where possible, but mainly find that people did their jobs and tended their communities, though sometimes grew angry and even hostile as they dealt with this film. My job is to explain events so that most actions seem reasonable and motivations clear, if often complex. I have yet to see evidence that anyone in these pages was guided by forces of evil.

The greatest weakness of this project results from the secrecy shrouding much of the production and certification, which filmmakers have yet to lift. With neither artists at Icon nor administrators in the Motion Picture Association of America (MPAA) making production files available (Gibson revealed financial information only when compelled by a judge), I must work with the film itself as publicly released, the marketing materials, journalists' reports and the occasional government record. The good news is that we have enough of those for several studies. But the reticence of Hollywood personnel to share the minutiae of development, shooting, post-production, market-strategizing, and classification renders some of this guesswork. I cite my sources and mark my guesses as such (e.g., 'presumably', 'apparently') in the pages that follow.

✕ Synopsis

Act One: In the Garden of Gethsemane, Jesus (James Caviezel) prays for strength and resists Satan's call to forsake the duty ahead. When Judas (Luca Lionello) betrays him to temple guards, loyal disciples do battle but cannot prevent the arrest. As Judas flees, disciple Peter (Francesco De Vito) wounds a temple guard, whom Jesus heals. Guards begin to beat Jesus; and across town his mother Mary (Maia Morgenstern) wakes with a sense of foreboding. Back in the garden, Judas is horrified to see Jesus suffer.

In the Jerusalem temple, priests and guards arrange a midnight trial. Mary and Magdalen (Monica Belluci) plead for help from soldiers, who alert their superiors that there may be trouble. In a flashback, Mary recalls a happy, young Jesus at work as a carpenter. In the Roman fort, the governor's wife Claudia (Claudia Gerini) awakes from a nightmare about assaults on Jesus; and Pilate (Hristo Naumov Shopov) learns from his right-hand man Abenader (Fabio Sartor) that the high priest Caiphas (Mattia Sbragia) is up to something.

A temple trial officiated by Caiphas results in more beatings and a conviction for blasphemy. Peter denies knowing Jesus to the hostile crowd. He recalls in a flashback that his master had foretold this betrayal, and begs Mary for forgiveness. Judas tries to return the blood money and begs priests for Christ's release, without success. As Mary senses her son imprisoned below, demons drive Judas from the city and from his senses. In the morning, he hangs himself.

Act Two: Judeans take Jesus to Pilate and accuse him of fomenting rebellion. Finding no cause, Pilate sends them to Herod (Luca De Dominicis) for judgment. Jesus says nothing to the decadent king, who sends him back. Meanwhile, Pilate complains to Claudia that he is powerless in the face of Caiphas's threats to incite unrest. Intimidated by the scornful priest as the trial of Jesus resumes, Pilate attempts to mollify the crowd. He first offers them the choice of whom to set free (they choose the killer Barabbas (Pietro Sarubbi)), and then orders Jesus scourged.

In the torture yard, a crowd of Judeans, including the priests, Mary, Magdalen and John (Christo Jivkov), gather to watch the punishment. Soldiers flagellate Jesus half to death. Claudia provides linens to the weeping women. In a flashback, Jesus recalls washing John's feet and warning them to be brave during their own persecutions. Abenader enters and angrily calls a halt, to prevent Jesus being killed. Afterward, Mary and Magdalen use the linens to mop up his blood. The latter recalls Jesus' rescue of her from a stoning. Soldiers mock Jesus with a robe and crown of thorns.

Back in the courtyard, Claudia watches in helpless anger as Caiphas, backed by an unruly crowd, once more intimidates a reluctant Pilate into condemning Jesus – this time to crucifixion.

Act Three: Jesus carries a huge cross through the streets of Jerusalem filled with hostile crowds. He falls several times from exhaustion as Mary and Satan keep pace. Mary embraces her fallen son, recalling a moment when he stumbled as a child. Abenader orders Jesus assisted, and soldiers recruit a reluctant Simon (Jarreth Merz) to help carry the cross. A sympathetic young woman gives Jesus a cloth to wipe his face. Simon objects to the soldiers' mistreatment of Jesus. Encouraged by Simon, Jesus sees the end of his road on the hill before them. He recalls his sermon on the mount and its lesson of love for all.

Act Four: Mounting Golgotha, Jesus further recalls the sermon in which he announced his plan to lay his life down. Simon leaves, unable to help. Soldiers strip and tie Christ to the cross, as he recalls his teachings of love and his divinity. As they nail him to the wood, Magdalen observes the miracle by which Jesus floats above the ground. As they raise the cross, John recalls the last supper and sharing of Christ's blood. Caiphas mocks Jesus and is rebuked by a crucified thief. An unrepentant thief scorns Jesus and is attacked by a crow in turn. Eventually, a storm blows up and drives priests from the site. A sympathetic guard gives Jesus some water. As Mary begs to die with her son, he tells her to go with John instead. As Jesus dies, the storm grows fierce, rending the temple curtain and floor, and forcing soldiers to hasten the execution. A fountain of water flows from Christ's body as a soldier pierces it with a spear. Caiphas weeps in despair, as does Satan in hell. Soldiers and Judeans depose the body, giving it to Mary to cradle. After some time, Jesus rises from his tomb, with no visible mark other than a hole in his palm.

✖ Part 1

PRODUCTION AND MARKETING

I first present the marketing of this movie as a series of criticisms exchanged between Icon Productions, a small group of scholars, a bigger group of pundits and reporters and a very large group of churches that responded to the media coverage and Gibson's entreaties – his sales pitches and claims to be persecuted for Christ – with an unprecedented moviegoing blitz.

I begin with the dispute between Icon and scholars over charges of anti-Semitism. I render this not as a pre-planned assault or simple bid for publicity, but as an initially unplanned spiral of events that built defensiveness on both sides, and which heightened tensions between all parties involved until well after the film's release.

I then add a view of this rancour as an all-but-inevitable conflict between competing professions that answer to the polarized extremes of large groups, which cannot easily accommodate each other's activities and goals. In the parts of the book to follow, I argue that this conflict disrupted the ways in which ratings boards and watchdog groups respond to screen violence.

It would be putting it mildly to write that Icon's spokespeople, headed by Mel Gibson, and several anti-defamation officials and scholars had a spat. Each accused the other of insensitivity and inflammatory rhetoric, of manipulation, and deceit, but also of endangering Jews. Each questioned the rights of the others to speak as they did, and each associated the other with global forces of destruction. I compile the most important links in this chain of events to show how group boundaries clarified as members traded insults, and how parties on both sides wrung solidarity, authority or money from the escalating fight.

The Turns of Events

In 1989, Mel Gibson used his wealth and clout to form the production company Icon with his business manager Bruce Davey. (They did this as a means to raise money so that Gibson could star in a film adaptation of *Hamlet*.) Gibson has since spoken of falling into despair in 1992, and of turning to the Catholicism of his youth. He reports having thought, at the time, of using Icon to film a passion; but he turned first to the stories of other martyrs. He directed and starred in *The Man without a Face* (1993) and then the 1995 blockbuster *Braveheart*, from which he gained more wealth and stature. Gibson finished the 1990s by acting in a series of action and family films (e.g., *Ransom* (1996), *Chicken Run* (2000)). In 2001, while portraying a Christian officer in the Vietnam movie *We Were Soldiers*, he had Icon producer Steve McEveety begin preparations to film *The Passion*. He acted in one more faith-themed film (*Signs* in 2002) and then set to work on production of *The Passion*. Relying on wealth generated by Gibson's hits, Icon financed the film without the aid of a major studio.

At McEveety's suggestion, Gibson called longtime acquaintance and screenwriter Benedict Fitzgerald, whose accomplishments included an adaptation of Flannery O'Connor's Christian-preacher story *Wise Blood* (1979). The two men agreed to focus on the last fifteen hours of the life of Christ, relying on gospels and such mystics as Anne Catherine Emmerich (2004) and Maria de Agreda (1971) as their primary sources. Fitzgerald recalled the faith of his childhood (which he would revive over the course of the production), added those memories to impressions from the mystics, and used them to draft a script (Shepherd *et al.*, 2004). Claiming to have allowed 'little deviation from the Synoptic gospels', Gibson then worked with Fitzgerald and eventually had the script translated into Latin and Aramaic by Loyola Marymount archaeologist Fr William Fulco. What resulted was a screenplay that avoided dependence on dialogue; focused attention on witnesses; incorporated Emmerich's medievalist contrast between sympathetic women and cruel Jewish men; and flashed back to rituals to establish the drama and violence as sacrament. The script would be religious in more than theme. Viewers were to experience the passion as ritual not just narrative, and feel redeemed by the suffering.

Over the course of 2002, Icon also readied for principal photography, which would take place in Italy over the fall and winter of 2002–3: first in the ancient towns of Craco and Matera (chosen for their streets and for Matera's vistas of ancient buildings), and then on the stages of Cinecittà in Rome. In September, as producers readied sets and assembled the company, Gibson held a press conference in Rome to announce his intent. He spoke of his devotional approach, of his wish to avoid subtitles for the Aramaic and Latin dialogue, of preparing to depict the violence in detail and of having found no distributor: 'I want to show the humanity of Christ as well as the divine aspect … . It's a rendering that for me is very realistic and as close as possible to what I perceive the truth to be' (quoted in Rooney, 2002, p. 26).

Most details of pre-production and principal photography, at least as they bear on the topic of this book, remain unavailable. Mel Gibson has alluded to 'opposition' on the set but offered few details (e.g., Neff, 2004, p. 32). Occasional interviews address conversations on set over the portrayal of Judean characters. They suggest that personnel came away with diverse impressions.

For instance, actor Ted Rusoff told the *Jerusalem Post* that he found the film inoffensive in respect of its portrayal of Judaism, but that

> Jewish audiences are likely to feel uncomfortable watching the film. A Jewish girl from Morocco [Evelina Meghnagi] who worked as an Aramaic dialogue coach … was highly incensed by the film's content. 'She kept buying bigger and bigger Stars of David to wear around her neck and kept flaunting them,' recalls Rusoff. And an Italian-Catholic actor who shared many of Rusoff's scenes was often outraged by what he perceived to be the film's anti-Semitic slant. Rusoff says the actor could not understand why Rusoff wasn't indignant as well. (Chartrand, 2004)

Fulco (quoted in Shepherd *et al.*, 2004) tells a different story. He describes Meghnagi as having been consulted by the director on the set with regularity, and having been heard on those occasions when she was offended:

> We kept running things by her. Mel would keep asking her, you know, 'Evelina, are you finding – What do you think of the way we are doing this scene, directing it?' And occasionally, she would say 'That's not the way we would do it.' … And occasionally, she would say 'That's – I find that very offensive' and Mel would sit down with her and work it out. He'd say 'Well, why? Why would it?' There were some things, for example, with the last supper, that – she said 'This is – You're bowdlerizing the Passover service.' And so Mel changed it. So he was very conscious about that all during the filming. And so we were really caught off guard with the barrage that followed right afterwards. Because, I think, Mel genuinely did his best.

Publicity materials for the film make frequent mention of piety and solidarity on the set, from morning mass to conversions of non-Christian cast and crew. But most details of script development, consultation with actors about their performances, and post-production editing are otherwise unavailable at this point. What we have in far greater supply are the public discussions of the film, upon which this book bears. That publicity began with the September press conference, and it grew the following year when Mel Gibson began to address American talk shows during the Roman shoot.

Apparently disturbed by a reporter's enquiries into his past and interview with his father Hutton, Mel Gibson complained to a friendly pundit (on *The O'Reilly Factor*, 14 January 2003) that dark forces aimed to subvert his film. Gibson linked the unnamed reporter to the 'enemies' with whom he would associate many critics of his film over the following year. Conservative pundits then elaborated that theory, of conspiracy against a fundamentalist entertainer, and defended Gibson from hypothetical criticism, through March.

On the sixth of that month, Gibson gave an interview to the conservative Catholic media outlet Zenit, as if anticipating the roles of Christians and Jews in the controversy to come. He spelled out the initial defence of his film as mere transcription of history:

> I'm telling the story as the Bible tells it. I think the story, as it really happened, speaks for itself. The Gospel is a complete script, and that's what we're filming. ... It's true that, as the Bible says, 'He came unto his own and his own received him not'; I can't hide that. But that doesn't mean that the sins of the past were any worse than the sins of the present. Christ paid the price for all our sins. The struggle between good and evil, and the overwhelming power of love go beyond race and culture. This film is about faith, hope, love and forgiveness. (Zenit, 2003a)

In such statements, Gibson set up two arguments that he would sustain over the following year: That any offensive depictions owed to gospel and history rather than to anti-Semitic intent, and that no account of Jewish guilt would be anti-Semitic anyway because it matters not who killed whom. In other words, while Jews served as principal, immediate causes for the execution on which the film dwells, that point is tangential to the gospel's message and the film's in turn – that we are all sinners and may be washed in Christ's blood. In his argument, one should not think Gibson anti-Semitic for describing liberal/Jewish conspiracies. His portrayals and accusations of liberal and Jewish aggression – whether of 2,000 years ago against Christ, or of today against Gibson himself – merely set the record straight in the spirit of forgiveness and truth.

Three days later, on 9 March, Christopher Noxon's article about Gibson-family Catholicism appeared in the *New York Times*. Noxon is the son of a neighbour of Gibson's church in Agoura Hills, and had been drawn to the topic by the construction of the large, movie-star-financed chapel so near to his father's house. He was the reporter who, during the Roman shoot, had interviewed Mel's father Hutton and so caused the younger Gibson's initial dismay (Silk, 2004).

Hutton Gibson is an author himself, of books critical of the post-Vatican II policy; and he shared with Noxon his doubts about Jewish accounts of the Holocaust and the state of the Roman Church. In his article, Noxon mentions that some traditionalists fix principal blame for the death of Christ on Jews, and that they reject as revisionism the Vatican orders on staging passions that will not inspire pogroms.

Upon reading this account of a Holocaust denier whose movie-star son filmed a passion for global release, and after hearing in addition that Gibson relied upon the anti-Semitic account of Emmerich's visions as he wrote his script, a few scholars resolved to look into the matter. That enquiry began in earnest when Eugene Fisher, Associate Director of Ecumenical and Interreligious Affairs (responsible for Catholic–Jewish relations) for the United States Conference of Catholic Bishops (USCCB) assembled an *ad hoc* committee of Catholic and Jewish scholars. This group would become infamous as Gibson's chief critics.

Fisher contacted Icon and exchanged a few notes with Fulco, whose attention to the script and service on the set put him in a position to comment on the depictions. In correspondence of 25 March (reported in Fredriksen, 2003, p. 26), Fulco assured his interlocutors that the script observed bishops' strictures on portrayals of Jews, and that the film – in rough-cut stage at the time – followed that script. He was not authorized to provide a copy.

Nevertheless, by late March, scholars on the committee had begun to raise public alarm. On the 28th, the *New York Jewish Week* reported comments by Michael Cook of Hebrew Union College, and Philip Cunningham of Boston College. The former said that 'Gibson's film may reverse progress the Christian community has made' in reinterpreting anti-Jewish New Testament passages. Cunningham likewise warned that, 'If the film violates these norms, I would anticipate a clear and explicit criticism of it from the Catholic magisterium throughout the world' (quoted in Greenberg, 2003a).

Two other members of Fisher's committee, apparently mindful of Icon's refusal to provide a script, voiced such concerns as the *Los Angeles Times* prepared a story for later in April: Anti-Defamation League official Eugene

Korn told a reporter that Gibson ought to share a look at his film: 'If he doesn't respond, the controversy will certainly heat up. We are all very vigilant about things like this.' And Union Theological Seminary teacher Mary Boys opined that,

> What we have here is a rich filmmaker whose beliefs may counter what the teaching of the church has been for the last 50 years … . He can get his views into the media and has far more power in that sense than what the church has. (quoted in Levine, 2004)

As that article was prepared for press, Fisher and his team waited for their chance to examine production materials directly. In mid-April, one arose. Fisher obtained a copy of a script through a friend, which issued from an anonymous source. (Icon's publicist later confirmed to the *New York Times* that this was an October 2002 shooting script, printed for use on the set in Matera (Goodstein, 2003, p. 10)). Fisher sent it to the scholars whom he had recruited, and informed Fulco on 17 April, in a letter that referred to the unnamed source as 'our Deep Throat'.

By this point, misunderstandings appear to have developed on both sides. Fisher later told his colleagues that he received no immediate request from Icon to return the script. And Icon personnel later told a reporter that they had believed themselves to be dealing with an official body of the Church (Boyer, 2003). It seems that each thought the scholars' review of the script was more fully authorized than it was. Meanwhile, the *Los Angeles Times* interviews with Korn and Boys appeared (on 22 April), featuring the criticism of Gibson and warnings of controversy quoted above. (The pace of events seems to have created a situation in which the publication of statements lagged behind actual progress, such that the *Los Angeles Times* writer did not know, by press date, that committee members had obtained copies of the script.)

While these scholars and officials read the shooting script, Gibson, Fulco and McEveety appear to have seen the *LA Times* article. Presumably, they pondered its implications for the public image of their work and grew concerned. On 24 April, they called Fisher and shared their sense that the committee was motivated by preconceptions to do 'a hatchet job' on the production, on the basis of a script never authorized for release. McEveety says that he told Fisher that 'whatever opinion you guys come up with are tainted notes' (Boyer, 2003). But scholars' committee member Paula Fredriksen, of Boston University, quotes Fisher as then intimating that Gibson was 'open to what we have to say', though 'still a bit cautious' (2003, p. 26). Misunderstandings help to escalate conflict; what appears to have been intended as a warning to back off was translated as a message to go ahead and compose a confidential report.

Though producers had expressed concern that scholars might do 'a hatchet job', the situation was probably worse than they imagined. As Fredriksen describes it, 'The script, when we got it, shocked us. Nothing of Gibson's published remarks, or of Fulco's and Gibson's private assurance had prepared us for what we saw' (2003, p. 27). In their report to Icon, the scholars responded with alarm and recommended massive changes to the film. In the context of the Israeli–Palestinian war, they wrote, they felt 'gravely concerned about the potential dangers of presenting a passion play in movie theatres' (Boys et al., 2003, p. 2). They took offence at the script's description of the Jewish mob as 'predatory', 'bloodthirsty', and 'frenzied', emitting 'hot, primitive noises, filled with animal anticipation', 'fueled by cruelty and the anticipation of painful torment and death' of Christ. They also noted descriptions of Caiphas as 'Smug. Arrogant', his eyes made 'shiny with breathless excitement' by the scourging of Christ. The report focused on the contrast between the portrayal of Pilate as intimidated by the mob and that of Caiphas as the schemer who rules over a temple so wicked that its adherents carve the cross on which Christ is to die (2003, pp. 11–13). In short, they wrote to Icon, the script seemed to depart from gospel accounts far enough to paint a picture of a predatory race. It confirmed the scholars' worst fears of a medievalist anti-Judaism fully revived. Their report concluded that the script required 'major revisions', without which the film would 'inflict serious damage and in all likelihood be repudiated by most Christian and Jewish institutions' (p. 6). According to Fredriksen's account (2003), the committee members integrated their individual reactions and prepared that report, to be shared with Icon directly and kept from the public eye. Fisher communicated the substance of the report to Fulco in late April and mailed it, in confidence, in early May (the report is dated 2 May).

In the days after receiving the report, Gibson appears to have moved quickly. He hired Christian publicist A. Larry Ross to publicize the scholars' complaints and Icon's response in a way that would appeal to evangelicals (Ross had worked as media director for evangelist Billy Graham for decades). Then, with a letter dated 9 May, Gibson had Icon threaten to sue the USCCB for stealing the script. Someone within Icon appears to have leaked the scholars' report to the conservative Catholic news service Zenit, which ran a story at the end of May that grouped the scholars' report with 'a string of recent attacks on Gibson's film' and noted that the committee 'disapproves of the film's treatment of the Gospel accounts of Jesus' passion as historical facts' (Zenit, 2003b). The Zenit story ended with a statement of support for Gibson by an archbishop: 'between a decent man and his critics, I'll choose the decent man every time – until the evidence shows otherwise'.

On 12 June, Gibson issued a press release to the Hollywood trade journal *Daily Variety* that refuted charges of anti-Semitism and expressed hope that his film would inspire rather than offend. In late June, he flew to the capital of conservative evangelicalism, Colorado Springs, where he screened his rough cut at Ted Haggard's New Life Church (Haggard was then president of the National Association of Evangelicals) and the headquarters of Focus on the Family. At his press conference that week, Gibson appealed to his potential supporters' goals as directly as possible, telling them that, 'The Holy Ghost was working through me on this film, and I was just directing traffic … I hope the film has the power to evangelize' (Dart, 2003, p. 14).

In the wake of these moves by Icon, scholars found themselves on the defensive. Fredriksen (2003) reports feeling hoodwinked, having kept the script in confidence and remained silent for a month only to find that Icon had taken the time to prepare a legal threat, a public statement and an oppositional campaign designed to bolster a filmed slander that could put the world's Jews at risk. People at Icon, in turn, felt that they had been conned by a bunch of academics posing as bishop's emissaries, who used a pilfered script to defame them and potentially cost the company tens of millions of dollars should the release flop. Each group had decided that the other worked in bad faith and to destructive ends. They had set the stage for a hostile drama that would last for months and serve to market the film.

That summer, Gibson continued to screen rough cuts to evangelical and other conservative groups, collecting statements of support and excluding the offended scholars and members of the Anti-Defamation League (ADL) who obviously wanted to see it and render further judgment. ('There is no way on God's green earth that any of those people will be invited to a screening. They have shown themselves to be dishonorable', Icon publicist Paul Lauer told the *New York Times* for an article published in early August (Goodstein, 2003, p. 10).)

In late July, the *New Republic* published Fredriksen's account of the squabble from the scholars' side. She concluded on an apocalyptic note:

> I shudder to think how *The Passion* will play once its subtitles shift from English to Polish, Spanish, or French, or Russian. When violence breaks out, Mel Gibson will have a much higher authority than professors and bishops to answer to. (2003, p. 29)

By the end of the defensive article, Fredriksen had drifted from careful account of the back-and-forth with Icon, and explanation of her scholar's paradigm, to warnings of calamities that one hears more often at rallies than at seminar tables.

Fellow professionals in journalism followed suit. In response to Icon and Ross's marketing, liberal pundits for such national papers as the *New York Times* and *Los Angeles Times* complained that Gibson had taken a hostile stance toward anyone who complained of anti-Semitism in order to promote the film to conservative groups that might themselves harbour anti-Jewish sentiments. For instance, Frank Rich (2003) complained, in the *New York Times* that,

Now sectarian swords are being drawn. The National Association of Evangelicals, after a private screening of 'The Passion,' released a statement last week saying, 'Christians seem to be a major source of support for Israel,' and implying that such support could vanish if Jewish leaders 'risk alienating two billion Christians over a movie.'

On 8 August, relations between Gibson and Jewish members of the scholars' committee worsened still. Eugene Korn told the *New York Jewish Week* that he had attended an Icon screening and argued with Gibson there, and that *The Passion* 'portrays Jews in the worst way as the sinister enemies of God' (Greenberg, 2003b, p. 1). Korn told the reporter that Gibson 'seems to be callous to the fear and concerns of the critics ... I came away with the feeling he's playing off the conservative Christians against the liberal Christians, and the Jews against the Christian community in general.' Arguing that Korn ought not have spoken to the press, and that by doing so he had violated the confidentiality agreement distributed and signed at Icon's screenings, publicist Lauer told the same reporter that 'The most important thing we are trying to do, which the ADL still has not recognized and is not cooperating [on], is trying to build a dialogue of understanding around the film.'

To complaints that he was Jew-baiting for publicity, and that evangelicals would spurn Jews in support of him, Gibson responded with more personal vitriol in the presence of a reporter, escalating public conflict further. (Boyer's September *New Yorker* profile quoted Gibson expressing his feelings about Frank Rich: 'I want to kill him', he said. 'I want his intestines on a stick. ... I want to kill his dog.') Gibson told the same reporter that

the acts against this film started early. As soon as I announced I was doing it, it was 'This is a dangerous thing.' There is vehement anti-Christian sentiment out there, and they don't want it. It's vicious. I mean,

I think we're just a little part of it, we're just the meat in the sandwich here. There's huge things out there, and they're belting it out – we don't see this stuff. … But we're called to the divine, we're called to be better than our nature would have us be. And those big realms that are warring and battling are going to manifest themselves very clearly, seemingly without reason, here – a realm that we can see. And you stick your head up and you get knocked.

Over the course of these public exchanges, which assigned import to the film and malice to opponents, *The Passion of the Christ* became a *cause célèbre*. Defensive gestures became self-fulfilling prophecies as group dynamics and emotional spirals led professionals into culture war.

Before I finish the story with the screenings of rough cuts and trailers in churches that winter, I pause to consider that, whatever the steps people took down this road, they may have been all but driven there by the way their organizations work – by disparate loyalties and professional routines. As commercial artists invested in free speech and courting a faith community, personnel at Icon worked to interpret holy texts in ways more enthusiastic than scholarly, and then to render truth on screen as melodrama rather than as disciplined history. By contrast, scholars serve different masters and maintain different values, and evangelical Christians others still. I turn next to these professions and communities, to suggest that their organizational goals may have exerted as much force as the cascade of events that I just reviewed.

The Needs of Groups

In August 2003, Gibson told the *New Yorker* that 'Inadvertently, all the problems and the conflicts and stuff – this is some of the best marketing and publicity I have ever seen' (Boyer, 2003). And Icon publicist Lauer said likewise to the *New York Times*: 'The controversy, he added, has built a considerable buzz about the movie. You can't buy that kind of publicity'

(Goodstein, 2003, p. 10). For such filmmakers, the debates recounted above were part of the job – using evangelical distaste for historicist scholarship to market their movie to churches.

Of her own profession, Professor Fredriksen (2004) noted that,

> My responsibility, meanwhile, is to speak up and speak out – not against the film so much as against the ignorance, and the unselfconscious anti-Judaism, that it so dramatically embodies and presents. Gibson has given myself and numberless colleagues in colleges, universities, and seminaries across the nation, a priceless opportunity for public education. Out of the ivory tower, past the Cineplex, into the churches and interfaith communities that have asked us all to come to speak. This teachable moment now serves as the silver lining that shines within the looming dark cloud of Gibson's *Passion*. (pp. 62–3)

Likewise, another scholars' committee member stated that, after the anger and chagrin of the previous year, 'as a teacher and a scholar, I am hopeful. Many organizations, institutions, and communities are using this controversy to stimulate dialogue, education, shared Scriptural study, and mutual respect' (Boys, 2004, p. 163). Like artists with works to sell to viewers, scholars pursue goals of our own – activities well served by debate over this film. Where Ross and Outreach used the conflict to market a movie, scholars used it to occasion new teaching and writing (like this book). Either way, professionals in combat were doing their jobs.

The *scholars* in question define their profession in terms of historical study of holy texts, conducted by degree-holding academics accountable to groups of their scholarly peers, in a stratified system dominated by Ivy League and other elite private and public schools. In the research that they share, the import of any line of holy writ depends on the contexts in which people wrote it rather than on God or its claim to truth. Levine (2004) urges those who discuss *The Passion of the Christ* to 'study the history of the period … try to understand why these Gospel accounts differ … know what sources are available to them to provide a fuller sense of Jesus' context' (p. 208). Meacham (2004) likewise argues that 'The Bible did not descend from heaven fully formed and edged in gilt. The writers of Matthew, Mark, Luke, and John shaped their narratives several decades after Jesus's death to attract converts' (p. 6).

As Reinhartz (2002) puts it in her study of the gospel of John, all of this 'creates a serious problem for readers for whom the Gospel has canonical and authoritative status' (p.100), which pretty much means that Biblical literalism has little place in most academic realms.[1] Scholars were essentially urging that literalists like Gibson not worship as they do but become more like scholars instead. Indeed, the *ad hoc* scholars' committee inadvertently provided Gibson's marketers with much of the ammunition that its appeal to evangelicals would aim at them. They accused the film's scenarists of 'failing to incorporate historical studies' of first-century Palestine (Boys *et al.*, 2003, pp. 4–5) and of writing as literalists instead, under the assumption that gospels were accurate, eyewitness testimony guided in translation by God. What scholars regard as anti-Jewish tracts written by partisan evangelists, decades after the events that inspired them, Gibson regards as, in a word, *gospel*. Scholars critiqued not only his hostile approach to the depiction of Jews but also a form of faith *per se*. By doing this, they made it easy for Gibson to change the subject and rally evangelicals to his defence.

Scholars regard passion plays as fit topics for their comment because they link them to medieval violence against European Jews. Recently consulted on productions of such films as *Judas* (2004) and *The Gospel of John* (2004), professionals in this network of historians and Bible scholars were growing accustomed to wielding authority over passion films (with the flattering attention that it could draw to their careers). To the *New Yorker* reporter who profiled Gibson in the fall of 2003, Fredriksen noted that, 'He doesn't even have a Ph.D. on his staff' (Boyer, 2003). That tone in scholarly rhetoric springs from a sense of duty and entitlement to speak with authority on matters of Biblical truth. What others see as matters of faith, are to such scholars matters of professionalism. What others felt as attacks on Christendom appeared to scholars to be them doing their jobs.

To such claims of authority over study of the Bible, Mel Gibson opposes a Priesthood-of-All-Believers literalism:

> They always dick around with it, you know? ... It's revisionist bullshit. And that's what these academics are into .... It was like they were more or less saying I have no right to interpret the Gospels myself, because I don't have a bunch of letters after my name. But they are for children, these Gospels. They're for children, they're for old people, they're for everybody in between. They're not necessarily for academics. Just get an academic on board if you want to pervert something! (quoted in Boyer, 2003)

In this respect, Catholic Gibson subscribes to a Protestant ethic of individual engagement with holy texts as opposed to submission to the authority of learned clerics or scholars. Each believer serves as her own priest, with no need of advanced education. This is not merely a professional artist's defence of freedom of speech (to which I return below) but it is also an evangelical ideal, defined by its ethic of personal duty to maintain a literal account of God's word.

Evangelicals maintain both strong beliefs (Biblical orthodoxy, the need to convert others and the importance of the crucifixion) and high levels of participation in conservative Protestant organizations. To such believers, the claims of scholars can have no privilege; and assertions that the gospels are anti-Semitic can seem like blasphemous nonsense that undermines the authority of their communities. As a leading evangelical journal put it, 'Christianity is incompatible with anti-Semitism' (*Christianity Today*, 2003, p. 43). From their perspective, no criticism of Jewish behaviour – from that implicit in their proselytizing Jews, to the more explicit blame for the condemnation of Christ – can be anti-Semitic, because Christians, by definition, cannot hate.[2] And no fidelity to gospel can be wrong because the holy text is, by definition, truth. Religious communities generate the solidarity that inspires commitment and maintains them by celebrating shared beliefs in stirring rituals (Marshall, 2002; Marvin and Ingle, 1999). Such rituals focus

on tales of miracles and gods, and are only diminished by scholarly discipline
and scientific scepticism. The needs of the two groups – scholars and
evangelical leaders – are distinct.

Finally, *filmmakers* have their own ties, based as they are in an industry
that affirms the protection of speech, hoping to forestall interference by the
state, to keep their market free and profits high. One expression of this
appeared in an editorial in *Daily Variety* (2003), which reframed the scholars'
committee work as a whisper campaign and defended the filmmakers as
artists:

> There already are cries of protest and dark insinuations of an anti-
> Semitic subtext. Writing in the current *New Republic*, Paula Fredriksen,
> an academic who has not seen the picture, suggests that release of 'The
> Passion' will have a dire impact. … These blatherings strike us as
> irresponsible. … As with all previous films depicting the period, some
> scholars and theologians will doubtless challenge Gibson's historical
> accuracy – indeed he is an actor, not a biblical scholar. But to condemn
> both the film and the filmmaker in advance reflects both bigotry and a
> disdain for free expression.

This statement from Hollywood's most widely read journal links believers'
freedom of faith to artists' freedom of speech, joining the interests of
filmmakers and worshippers. Indeed, to filmmakers, religious groups are
useful as marketing agents as long as they make no other demands. Icon asked
Ross, Outreach and the other firms to sell the film as a way to evangelize,
tying its fortunes to theirs. What filmmakers hoped would raise their profits
could equally well serve as a tool to boost churches' growth.

By contrast, filmmakers have little use for scholars, who can neither
raise ticket sales nor lobby hard enough to inspire censorship. Though they
can make trouble for major corporations should they forge ties with more
effective groups (as the scholars' committee did when it included anti-
defamation personnel), Icon is an independent producer with few ties to a

larger conglomerate, and was free to defy scholars' demands and make whatever film it could afford to see flop (which failure, until the first week of release, remained a sobering prospect). Bolstered by profits from Gibson's hits, it was even more able than a major studio to flout pressure groups to whom it did not need to sell its film (or whom it could use as symbols of unchristian evil in an oppositional campaign). As a result, the filmmakers had little reason to make peace with scholars, every reason to approach evangelicals, and so mostly invoked filmmaker ideals of free expression and evangelical notions of piety.

Given all of this, it remains difficult to imagine how filmmakers could have come to much agreement with scholars over this film. Icon had no motive for rejecting either free expression or orthodoxy in favour of scholarly authority. The professional ties were so radically different that even the most deliberate conversations, conducted by the most patient and sensitive parties, might never have aligned their views. They served their professional needs by avoiding common ground.

The Final Push

The night before the film opened, MSNBC reported that

> None of the major studios wanted to touch 'The Passion of the Christ' when Mel Gibson first proposed the idea. Now, many of them probably wish they had. Word of mouth on the movie has spread like, well, the gospel. And it's drawing flocks of moviegoers into theaters. Part of that is due to a marketing campaign unlike anything Hollywood has ever seen. (Cobb, 2004)

Though the campaign differed from its predecessors in respect of Gibson's polarizing wrath, Icon otherwise followed a path beaten decades before. Cecil B. DeMille marketed his 1927 silent *The King of Kings* to women's groups and churches across the country, at a time when the Motion Picture Producers and Distributors of America courted Christian and Jewish groups in attempts to avoid outcry and the censorship that public outrage might inspire (Maltby, 1990).

Paramount followed suit in 1933, on behalf of its wide release of DeMille's *The Sign of the Cross* (a film about first-century Christians). Its business model instructed marketers:

> Church-goers! Here the appeal is tremendous. Reach this class thru the clergy, thru sermons, thru direct mail. … DON'T MIX YOUR ISSUES! REMEMBER: DRAMA AND THUNDER AND SEX FOR THE GENERAL PUBLIC … RELIGIOUS APPEAL FOR THE CHURCHES … . (quoted in Hall, 2002, p. 174)

In that case, Catholic outrage over sexual display in the film's scenes of Roman revelry created publicity problems for filmmakers that helped to inspire an era of strict regulation in Hollywood (Walsh, 1996).

United Artists and famed director George Stevens tried it again in the early 1960s, when publicizing *The Greatest Story Ever Told* (1965), which quickly became UA's biggest failure of the period (Hall, 2002, p. 170). Stevens lauded the Christian character of major actors, especially of Max Von Sydow, who played Christ; criticized previous efforts and promised that his would be different; and appealed directly to churchgoers for patronage. He resolved that the 'public must consider it a privilege to buy tickets to our picture' (p. 174), and pursued this goal by seeking for commendations (for himself as well as for his film) from virtually every civic and religious group he could think of (p. 175).[3] By that time, the strategy for marketing a movie about Christ was well established, even if it had a poor track record.

In December 2003, Christian publicity company Outreach began to show copies of a more finished print and a trailer for *The Passion of the Christ* to church groups. Its marketers encouraged churches to distribute ads to members and to potential converts, and to book in advance as many screenings as possible (a strategy they were to repeat with sales of the video the next summer, urging churches to buy in bulk). Its campaign encompassed viral emails linked to trailers, which youth could send to their friends; websites that offered movie-themed sermons to pastors; minor-release forms for parents who wanted to send their children to the R-rated movie in the US; and ways to obtain mundane ads such as booklets, posters, postcards and so forth. Icon licensed tie-in merchandise to be carried by thousands of Christian speciality stores, ranging from pewter nail pendants to coffee-table books of photos from the set. It also licensed co-op commercials, with which, for a bit less than $800, a church could advertise both the film and its services on local television. In its appeal to church groups, Icon followed long-established rules of marketing movies about Christ.

However, this marketing campaign differed from its predecessors in respect of its embrace of the conflict that studios generally try to avoid. According to Caldwell's account (2004), Outreach appealed to the many conservatives who saw in Icon's critics a force hostile to Christendom:

> As a result, conservatives spent a lot of time in adrenaline-rush counterattack mode. The scholars, Abraham Foxman of the Anti-Defamation League, and even *New York Times* columnist Frank Rich seemed almost to blunder, unknowing, into this other reality. (p. 215)

Scholars had played into the Manichean sense of opposition upon which group solidarity thrives, and Outreach took full advantage.

Anti-Defamation League officials contributed, perhaps unwittingly, to the campaign by maintaining their criticism of the film. In January, the *New York Times* reported that Foxman had complained of the selective enforcement of Icon's confidentiality agreement, which supporters of the film were free to ignore: ('pastors and church leaders are free to speak out in support of the movie and your opinions resulting from today's exposure to this project and its producer', the contract is reported to have read (Kennedy, 2004, p. 12). Such negative commentary on the film kept it in the headlines and Gibson in many evangelicals' sympathetic thoughts. 'The church was an active ingredient in the movie's success because people got their friends and families excited about it – and then Abe Foxman did the rest', Outreach told Caldwell (2004, pp. 215–16). Evangelicals and Catholics in Colorado Springs discussed the controversy surrounding the film and told a reporter of 'a growing Christian defensiveness over a perceived Jewish assault on their faith … their sense of cultural siege' (Halevi, 2004, p. 21).

Indeed, the warnings by critics turned to grist for conservative mills. According to Hollywood critic Michael Medved, who had long taken Hollywood to task for its liberalism, 'the attacks on an unseen movie reflected the predominantly liberal political orientation of the ADL and other groups that represent the Jewish establishment' (2004, p. 39). Supporters of the film likened critics to liberals – forces to counter by supporting the film.

Introducing his film to crowds on his roadshow campaign, Gibson offered stories of his faith, his sense that God was with him on the set and that evil forces had aligned themselves against him. Crowds appear to have been moved; and the result was a rare level of excitement about a film, the sort of saturation-level awareness and in-group commitment of which Hollywood's marketers dream. The *Dallas Morning News* reported that:

> Owing to Mel Gibson's wariness of mainstream media, his fear of what he calls 'the anti-Christian sentiment out there' and a one-of-a-kind faith-based marketing campaign, his movie *The Passion of the Christ* is expected to make a triumphant entry into theaters … . By courting evangelical Christians and selectively pre-screening *The Passion* for thousands of pastors, religious broadcasters, Catholic priests, church leaders and conservatives, Icon has whipped up advance ticket demand. Church members across the country are buying tickets in bulk; one member of Prestonwood Baptist has purchased all the seats for early-morning Ash Wednesday screenings at the 20-screen Cinemark Tinseltown in Plano. (Sumner, 2004)

In the wake of the withdrawal by Fox from the distribution of the film back in the fall of 2003, Icon had reached out to the Regal Entertainment group, which had been purchased that year by conservative Christian Philip Anschutz. Regal arranged private group screenings on a mass basis, selling out whole theatres to churches. Upon the film's release in late February, the combination of mass bookings by church groups and the widespread publicity afforded by public debate met the conditions of a blockbuster event. The goal of blockbuster marketing is to place a film in as many theatres as possible on opening weekend; saturate mass media with mentions of the film in the weeks prior to release; and try to create a synergistic effect in which the opening weekend becomes an event motivating people to see it right away in order to participate in conversations with their friends (Gomery, 2003). The size of the opening weekend's business tends to determine the size of its worldwide gross. In most respects, the release of *The Passion of the Christ* followed this model, though the box office outside the US failed to live up to expectations set by its opening stateside (to which point I return in Part 3).

On the eve of the film's release, just before Icon ordered media silence among its marketing spokespeople, Gibson gave final interviews. To the *Los Angeles Times*, he emphasized his sense of persecution:

> His film is on the verge of release, and even the outraged criticism seems to be buoying it toward a big opening. Yet Gibson is not happy. 'I'm subjected to religious persecution, persecution as an artist, persecution as an American, persecution as a man,' he says. 'These things have happened in the last year. I forgive them all. But enough is enough. They're trying to make me some cult wacko. All I do is go and pray. For myself. For my family. For the whole world. That's what I do.' (Abramowitz, 2004, p. A1)

Thus did Gibson conclude the most successful church-based promotion in the history of cinema. What had disappointed DeMille and failed for Stevens would finally succeed for *The Passion of the Christ*. Instead of opening to critical yawns and tepid crowds, this film had become a moral cause, its status as cultural event secured by the conflict between the professional groups and the marshalling of evangelicals to support one side.

The next step would be taken by the many boards around the world that rate or censor films for national consumption. I argue, in this next part, that religious interest in this film spurred censors to alter their decisions.

✖ PART 2

RATING AND CENSORSHIP

The Passion of the Christ features two show-stopping, set-piece scenes of torture, in which assailants show glee as they deliver blows with canes, flagella, hammers and nails. In the United States, the Classification and Rating Administration (CARA) had long maintained standards for R-rated films that exclude such action. It had required filmmakers who sought R ratings to cut repeated strikes with weapons, especially those accompanied by expressions of pleasure.[4] But CARA gave *The Passion of the Christ* that R rating ('for sequences of graphic violence') with these scenes intact. And it did this while other boards either restricted viewing to adults (in the United Kingdom, Spain and Mexico), to those over sixteen (Netherlands, Quebec and Germany),[5] to Christians in churches (Malaysia); or banned the film altogether (China, Bahrain and Kuwait).

As an example of a more restrictive rating, against which the US certification stands in such contrast, consider the UK. Against the request of Icon for a 15 rating, the British Board of Film Classification (BBFC) upheld

Screen capture: Jesus lies in a pool of blood after ten minutes of torture.

its standards. Those state that, 'Violence may be strong but must not dwell on the infliction of pain and injury.' In a guide intended to make the board accountable to the public that it serves, the Students' BBFC site (SBBFC) describes its negotiation over this film:

> There were arguments mounted for both '15' and '18', but after extensive discussion the majority view, and the view of the Presidents and Director was that the strong bloody violence, particularly the extended and brutal whipping scene in which the character Jesus is repeatedly lashed for over 10 minutes, were [sic] just too strong for the '15' category. It was also felt that, given the realism of the make up and special effects, and the strong sustained sadism of the soliders [sic] carrying out the whipping, along with the close-up detail of injury and blood during this and the crucifixion scene, audience expectations of violence at '15' would be challenged by the work. (SBBFC, 2009)

The announcement of this decision in the UK was uncontroversial. With no strong Christian demand for wide availability, the BBFC simply treated the violence as it would in any other film. In an interview with a fan site, an officer of the BBFC elaborated that,

> obviously support for the Church of England is not as strong as it was. So, in terms of public opinion it's not a huge factor. With *The Passion of the Christ*, the religious angle didn't motivate our decision to a great extent; we focused on the violence, which is why we gave it an '18'. (SBBFC, 2009)

On only one occasion did a nation with an actively religious populace restrict screenings to that extent and for that reason. On 10 March, Mexico's General Directorate of Radio, Television and Cinematography (RTC)

> slapped an adults-only rating on 'The Passion of the Christ' ... infuriating Twentieth Century Fox Films. ... Fox Mexico general director Juan Jose

Hernandez was outraged at the news, which came shortly after a private screening of 'Passion' for Catholic officials. 'This hasn't happened in any country in the world,' he said. … Hernandez has demanded an explanation from classification board the RTC and has filed an appeal. He wants a B-15 rating, the rough equivalent to a PG-13. (Bensinger, 2004, p. 8)

The film would go on to be a modest hit in Mexico that year (albeit, not on the level of sequels to *Harry Potter*, *Spider-Man* or *Shrek*); but the rating itself (based on the film's 'high degree of violence') appears to have been felt as a slap: 'Gibson reportedly told the Mexican press that the rating bestowed on his film upset him, noting that movies such as "Terminator 3" received a more lenient rating' (Peterson, 2004). Fox appealed the rating, a day after its announcement, but without success.

In other nations, religious groups – Christian and otherwise – made stronger claims and influenced boards to alter their decisions in order to grant the film wider release. In order to demonstrate that relationship, I focus on the last stage of the film's marketing and the first stage of its release – its reception by national censors and boards of review. It begins at the ground zero of Hollywood, home of the titanic industry in which the film was produced and first rated. It then offers more contrasting cases from other nations, which suggest what might have happened in the US had its ratings administration not made an exception to its rule. I suggest that the strength of a nation's religious groups could help to determine whether a film board would follow its usual practice in the restriction of religious iconography or graphic violence.

Deference in Hollywood

A review of the Los Angeles-based industry of which Icon is a part allows us to see this film's release within the context of a century of Hollywood regulation. CARA is the board that affixes G, PG, PG-13, R and NC-17 ratings to most films and videos destined for cinema and home-video release within the United

States. It is the principal form of regulation in Hollywood, founded by the Motion Picture Association of America in 1968 with the support of the National Association of Theatre Owners (NATO). The MPAA is a trade association composed of major studios (Disney, Paramount, Sony, Twentieth Century-Fox, Universal and Warner Bros.); and NATO controls most cinema screens. This means that, in order to gain wide release within the US, a producer must submit to regulation by those most likely to profit from major studio releases.

Regulation is an economic matter in Hollywood. Walsh (1996) documents the financial self-interest behind the acceptance of a Production Code of onscreen ethics by major studios back in 1930 (they had been threatened with a takeover by the Federal Trade Commission, harassed by regional censorship and left vulnerable by the stock-market crash of 1929). Only with a highly publicized, church-approved mechanism of self-censorship could studios operate free of regulation. As Sandler (2007) shows, the major studios created CARA in 1968 for similar reasons, though in an environment less dominated by sectarian groups. CARA became the gateway through which product would have to flow on its way to widespread distribution; and major studios kept that channel open to the massive youth market by assuring parents that the films that CARA rated were basically safe for the age groups specified. By continuing to supplant the regulatory power of the government (which might be inclined toward more open competition by independent producers), the six studios that belong to the MPAA could maintain oligopolistic control over the distribution pipeline. Taking advantage of that control, Sandler shows, CARA has demonstrated systematic bias against submissions not produced by the major studios. That is, similar depictions submitted from outside the MPAA receive more restrictive ratings and, as a consequence, smaller and less competitive releases. The MPAA uses CARA to maintain its market advantage.

Independently produced experiments in restricted (NC-17-rated) filmmaking have caused scandals for their distributors and the MPAA without even providing compensatory profit. Sandler (2007) suggests that MPAA studios learned from such experiments that controversy had little upside and could threaten their family-friendly brand. As a result, MPAA studios have abandoned many controversial projects that might have inflamed pressure groups; and CARA tends not to indulge independent filmmakers who push the envelope of allowable offence. It appears that for such reasons Twentieth Century-Fox declined to distribute *The Passion* (as the film was titled in August 2003) despite its first-look agreement with Icon. The filmmakers eventually signed a distributor (Newmarket) less vulnerable to public pressure, one with no other corporate holdings that angry crusaders might boycott (Smith, 2003). For this reason, one might have expected CARA to brand the explicit depiction of torture with an NC-17 rating, implicitly pressuring filmmakers to trim footage in order to obtain a more saleable R. Issuing as it did from an independent company, without the cooperation of a major studio, one would have expected *The Passion of the Christ* to draw a particularly restrictive response.

Furthermore, the MPAA was recovering from damage to its reputation sustained when the Federal Trade Commission caught it marketing violent entertainment to children in 2000, in the wake of a series of widely publicized shootings in American high schools. The MPAA responded to the scandal by reducing its flow of R-rated movies and by imposing greater restriction on its filmmakers. Likewise, NATO enforced its age-based admission policies more strictly (Sandler, 2007, p. 202). They mostly left depictions of graphic violence to independently produced films with NC-17 ratings, and relegated those to smaller numbers of screens where they would generate little profit or fuss.

For these reasons, Hollywood had been moving away from graphic depictions of violence on screen when Icon submitted its work. It is in this context that we must ask why CARA granted *The Passion of the Christ*, with its unprecedented scenes of extensive torture, an R rating.

Support for Violence

Two trends seem most likely to explain CARA's decision. First, lengthy torture scenes may have become more acceptable at the R-rated level as the US went to war and inspired debate over torture in its 'War on Terror'. CARA bills itself as reflecting community standards; and, just as World War II inspired the Production Code Administration (PCA) to allow depiction of knife and bayonet violence, and the Vietnam war era saw the PCA displaced by the less restrictive CARA, the Iraq war may have expanded CARA's tolerance for images of savagery on screen.

Stephen Prince (2003) and David Slocum (2005) have documented how Hollywood filmmaking during World War II altered to help augment the generation of solidarity, both by contrasting American discipline to Japanese savagery and bodily harm, and also by allowing some vivid depictions of violence against US soldiers, 'especially when that could help dramatize the difficulty and the importance of wartime effort and sacrifice' (Prince, 2003, p. 159). Prince also notes that the founder of CARA, Jack Valenti, invoked the turmoil of war in his defence of the relaxation of restrictions on violence by the MPAA in 1968, during which time the US military was heavily involved in conflict in Vietnam. Valenti emphasized 'how filmmakers were inevitably responding to, and reflecting, a revolution in social mores that was underway in the larger culture, a defense that implicitly acknowledges the economic incentives for filmmakers to mirror these changes on screen' (Prince, 1998, p. 25). In this way, wartime focus on actual death has twice served as licence for studios to market bloodshed on screen.

By 2004, the US found itself in a similar situation: recovering from the national trauma induced by the broadcast of death on September 11 2001, and involved in two wars and a national debate on the use of torture. It seems likely that these events had effects on deliberations within CARA (which records are unavailable at this time) similar to those that earlier wars had had on the PCA. Hollywood regulation is market-driven and can shift with government pressure and national mood. Widespread discussion of torture and maiming can lead to more graphic depiction on film, especially those portrayals that foreground suffering for one's nation. In this way, the larger context of the release of *The Passion of the Christ* probably favoured its success, with boards of certification and with audiences.

A second trend appears also to have affected CARA's rating of this film – the way in which this release differed from others in respect of the parties supporting it. Releases can be sullied when large groups protest demeaning portrayals of their members, which has made conglomerates shy away from offending them. The party *complaining* of unfavourable depiction in this case consisted of Jews wary of anti-Semitic stereotypes, and a small group of scholars who tried to exert their authority. But Icon was not merely another independent company pushing an artistic envelope within the studio-controlled system, and so could not be so easily discouraged with a restrictive rating. Icon, in its struggle to overcome the complaints of scholars and other watchdogs of anti-Semitism, had the backing not of a studio invested in avoiding controversy but of a far larger group that also claimed aggrieved status, which courted controversy and threatened to incite the very outcry that the MPAA wishes to avoid. Though CARA does not share evidence of its deliberations, it is worth considering the extent to which widespread evangelical Christian support for *The Passion of the Christ* may have made it easier to justify a lenient R rating.

Consider the deep background to growing debate over *The Passion of the Christ*, which included imputations of anti-Semitism and prurient spectacle on the one side, and charges of anti-Christian persecution on the other. Hollywood has been there before. Sixteen years prior, another passion play ignited a firestorm when conservative Christians took on another Catholic filmmaker. The release, in 1988, of *The Last Temptation of Christ* (discussed further in Part 5), was notable in part for the open expression of hostility toward Jews in Hollywood that it inspired. Attempts to stop that release included anonymous threats of violence, censorious moves by governing bodies and withdrawal by a nationwide cinema chain (Lyons, 1996). Universal Studios learned that such controversy can disrupt its business. Presumably, the lesson contributed to the majors' increasing tendency to avoid any prospect of injurious debate.

I showed in the preceding part that conservative pundits joined filmmakers in describing the scholars and Jewish spokespeople as leading edges of a force arrayed against Christ, which they saw as attempting to do to Gibson what ancient Judeans had done to their Lord. Did CARA defer to Christians in order to keep a profitable peace in 2004? Famed critic Roger Ebert opined as much in his review of the film:

> The MPAA's R rating is definitive proof that the organization either will never give the NC-17 rating for violence alone, or was intimidated by the subject matter. If it had been anyone other than Jesus up on that cross, I have a feeling that NC-17 would have been automatic. (2004)

The *Los Angeles Times* likewise speculated that

> the R designation also may cast renewed attention on the Motion Picture Assn. of America ratings system and raise questions about whether any kind of violence would be sufficient to warrant an NC-17. The rating has largely been applied to movies with explicit sexual content. (Munoz, 2004)

Though neither Ebert nor the *Times* reporter acknowledge it, filmmakers have trimmed scenes of assault and torture, after first failing to secure R ratings, for decades. Filmmakers have reported, and documented with video releases of before-and-after cuts of their footage, that the MPAA slaps the more restrictive NC-17 ratings on early drafts of films on a regular basis. Contractually bound to obtain Rs or PG-13s, editors trim such scenes to satisfy CARA. The question, then, is not whether CARA regulates violence, but why it did not do so in this case. Because CARA cloaks deliberations, one can only speculate what factors bore on its judgment. Because it never rated *The Passion of the Christ* NC-17, we have no record of comment against the MPAA's handling of the release and no direct way to test Ebert's theory.

We do have a contrasting example, however – an immediately subsequent and parallel case in New Zealand. There, the Office of Film and Literature Classification (OFLC) offended the film's Christian supporters by according it a restrictive rating, which barred anyone younger than sixteen from viewing the film. One learns rules by listening to complaints about their violation because, on those occasions, offended parties spell them out. The New Zealand story is worth recounting for its delineation of the role of Christian groups as supporters of this film, as they made their case for showing children the torture of Christ.

Defiance in New Zealand

Two days after receiving a copy of *The Passion of the Christ*, New Zealand's Chief Censor of Film and Literature, Bill Hastings, told a reporter that he intended to restrict showings to persons sixteen and older. A few days later (on 20 February 2004), his office did just that, citing the film's 'Brutal violence, torture and cruelty'.

Within hours of that announcement, the forewarned Christian Society for the Promotion of Community Standards (SPCS) filed an appeal. In a statement the following week, it argued against such strict regulation on the logic that,

> parents and guardians are more than capable of making informed decisions about the suitability of children under the age of 16 years attending this film. They all have prior warning of the violent aspects to the storyline and depictions via the film's descriptive note. (SPCS, 2004a)

The Society also urged that younger teens be admitted,[6] and that families rather than the government take responsibility for regulation, because the film tells a story of historical and religious merit:

> The Society believes that the story of the last 12 hours of the life of Jesus and His subsequent Resurrection is of such a high level of significance, historically, culturally, socially and spiritually, that many teenagers at

high school aged 13–15 would want to see this film and would greatly benefit from seeing it. … [I]t is central to our country's Judeo-Christian heritage. (SPCS, 2004a)

The Society's secretary emphasized these twin points about non-fiction and his subculture's importance to its nation when he told the New Zealand Press Association that the death of Christ 'was possibly the most significant event in the history of Western society' and that the film's graphic violence was 'justified by several accounts of Christ's death'. He asked the OFLC to reclassify *The Passion of the Christ* as 'an educational film, open to accompanied viewers as young as 13' (New Zealand Press Association, 2004b).

At this point, in a mirror image of Gibson's belligerence in the face of challenge, Chief Censor Hastings suggested that 'if I was to reconsider it, I might reconsider it up' (New Zealand Press Association, 2004b). He reiterated the standard of violence invoked by such ratings boards; he had restricted the film, he said, because its victim is attacked in such a repeated and relentless manner, and this is graphically depicted on screen. That is, he cited the usual workings of his office, arguing that any such scene of bloody torture would earn such a rating.

The appeal before the Film and Literature Board of Review (FLBR) took place in March as the film played to adult-only crowds. It was supported by the combination of hundreds of evangelical churches as well as by an organ of the Catholic Church, though it was filed in the name of the NZ movie distributor Hoyts. The appeal maintained the Society's emphasis on the tie between culture and Christendom: 'The classification of the Classification Office of R16 with a descriptive note "*Brutal violence, torture and cruelty*" is too restrictive compared to overseas Christian-based English speaking countries [Australia, USA, and Ireland] (FLBR, 2004, p. 3). It also noted the link between stories of sectarian and national sacrifice in seeking

a classification of R15, which is the same classification as '*Saving Private Ryan*' which contains '*graphic realistic war scenes*'. Described by the retired President of the US MPAA Censorship Authority as a film that should be seen by every American young person, because it would show them the 'cost of our redemption' as a nation. (p. 6)

To support this point about graphic violence, as justified by its role in redemptive sacrifice, the appeal 'refers to other passages in scripture that predict the intense suffering of Christ for the purpose of expiating sin' (p. 7).

For all of this theological argument, appellants took exception to the notion that they merely sought favour for Christians. Referring to Roger Ebert's theory that the MPAA was intimidated by the subject matter (quoted above), appellants argued that,

Here, he panders to the shallow and misguided insinuations, rarely voiced, that somehow censors are being forced to show a degree of religious favouritism in granting the film its current US classification. It is stating the obvious that a film with over-riding cultural, historical, artistic and religious significance commands a consideration by censors on a different level to a mere 'smut movie'. The same argument applies regardless whether or not the central figure is Jesus, or any other highly significant historical person. (FLBR, 2004, p. 8)

The desire is for deference not to Christianity alone, on this argument, but to any subculture vital to the nation and to the recognition of Christianity as one of those. Appellants claimed that their interests were not 'special' but were those of the nation instead.

In his response at this board of review, Chief Censor Hastings not only reiterated that he had gone about business as usual in rating the film, but also countered this cultural-significance argument, directly refusing to grant the deference demanded by Christian groups: 'A classification below 16 could also be seen to privilege one religion ahead of others on the basis that the film's depictions are historically accurate, a basis that is in fact contested' (FLBR, 2004, p. 15). Hastings suggests that Christians merit no subcultural privilege but must suffer instead the indignity of seeing graphic depictions of sacrifices for their group classified as the board would a horror film or pornography. He counters the truth claims that define the group and treats the foundation of their faith as akin to any fiction. Offended by this line of argument, appellants rejected

> the Chief Censor's alleged statement on News Talk ZB that the film fits the '*horror*' category. It is irresponsible to claim this film fits the same genre as '*The Exorcist*' and '*Rosemary's Baby*' as allegedly stated by the Chief Censor. (p. 7)

To contemporary evangelical Christian groups, such comparison of the gospels to horror scripts and entertainment can amount to a frontal attack by secular officials who have already assumed so much of the authority that once belonged to religion. Just as the secular drift of central government over the last few centuries sapped sects of their arms and political force (Bruce, 1996), the rise of commercial media removed most storytelling from their purview. Secular government and profit-driven corporations ('mass media', in common parlance) have assumed many of the storytelling functions and authority once served and enjoyed by sectarian groups. These trends pushed sects to the margins of what they regard as their own national culture. Today, I suggest, one point of subcultural protest is to secure deference from government and the culture industry, and so to restore some of that status. Hastings, an officer of the New Zealand state, waved that demand away.

In its reply to this affront, the Society appears to have been willing to set aside its fundamentalist claims to truth (and its historical justification for the depiction of violence). But Hastings's comparison of the film – a faithful rendering of its foundational narrative of sacrifice – to a low-brow genre such as horror appears to have given greater offence. Its response was as stern as scholars' critiques of the movie have been. In its bid for wider release of the film, the appeal characterized critique of *The Passion of the Christ* as tantamount to scorn for Christendom.[7] It quoted famed Jewish editor Leon Wieseltier's *New Republic* editorial to reply that,

It is not surprising that many who show disdain and contempt towards
the Christian message of sacrifice, hope and forgiveness found in
Jesus Christ, will try and vilify any attempt to realistically portray the
death of Christ, as some sort of 'repulsive masochistic fantasy' and
deride this film as 'a sacred snuff film'. (quoted in FLBR, 2004, p. 8)

The appellants' defensive response to Wieseltier's 'snuff film' charge – the
association of the passion with particularly low entertainment – is worth
pursuing for a moment, because it suggests how people decide what to censor
– how group membership shapes responses to this film.

Titillation

The term 'snuff film' refers to a legend of young women cast in pornography
and killed on screen for the amusement of viewers (Brottman, 1997; LaBelle,
1980). Discussion of such legendary murder, ostensibly committed for the
enjoyment of sadists, frames it as the type of film most deserving censorship –
an extreme of generic entertainment invoked to bolster regulation. By
reference to the term in his panning of *The Passion of the Christ*, Wieseltier
(2004, p. 19) implies that a decent society might suppress or at least condemn
such footage, whatever the motives its creators might have. For the purpose of
exploring the logic of the appeal to the restrictive New Zealand rating, I
consider his comparison and the appellants' reply.

First, both snuff films, in appearing to show actual killings, and filmed
passions, in recreating the same, present graphically realistic murders for their
audiences. Each involves sacrifice for a group in a carnal display of cruelty and
invites viewers to measure their well-being in terms of the suffering shown:
many Christians regard grace as a gift bought with Christ's pain, and
feminists hold that violence against women can affirm the privileges of men
(Caputi, 1989; LaBelle, 1980; MacKinnon, 1989). That is, where the
crucifixion was meant to ransom doomed souls – permitting Christ to suffer

so that grateful sinners go free – sexual murder would allow male viewers to revel in their oppressive might and savour the helplessness of women to resist. In both cases, the suffering of the victims is crucial to the ritual's effect.

Focusing on symbols of sacrifice, rituals can generate *solidarity*, the pride taken in group membership that runs as the emotional lifeblood through human groups (Marvin and Ingle, 1999). The lesson of such ritual is that the group is so deserving that valued gifts (precious livestock, legions of youth, revered heroes) shed blood for its sake. Stirred by the carnage and assured of their worth, onlookers can feel pride in belonging, by whatever name they call it: patriotism, brotherhood, fellowship. This emotional payoff empowers groups to make demands on their members and therefore to flourish.

It would be putting it mildly to say that the appellants in New Zealand took exception to comparison of their ritual narrative to a snuff fantasy. Their appeal objected to description of *The Passion of The Christ* as a snuff movie and states

> The pained agony of those of Jesus' followers who witness the events as depicted in the film and deal [*sic*] with in the Gospel accounts, is a clear echo of the pain his followers of today do feel (and give testimony to), recounting and reflecting upon the events of his Passion. It is perverse in the extreme to suggest that a high level of excitability and titillation in the minds of Christians is the intended purpose of this film, or indeed is the result from viewing of this film. No balanced reviewer has suggested this. (FLBR, 2004, p. 8)

The goal of a balanced review, in the Society's argument, is to tell the difference between the kinds of pleasure gleaned from viewing the sacrifice. Its logic follows that of wartime propaganda, in which it is claimed that one's nation goes to war with reluctance and regret for the death that results, but that enemy nations wage war with pleasure and squander their soldiers' lives (Marvin and Ingle, 1999). In this logic, a 'good' group (Christians watching a passion, in this case) reveres the sacrificial hero and endures its aversion to the sight of his pain only to know the extent of his love. By contrast, the 'bad' group scorns the victim sacrificed, feels no aversion to the carnal display, but revels instead in the suffering caused for its sake. One's own group complains that the other enjoys its *titillation*, and distinguishes this good art from the debasement of porn.

Some evangelical critics of *The Passion of the Christ* approve the use of violence to move viewers. A critic for the American journal *Plugged In* (an organ of the conservative watchdog organization Focus on the Family) writes,

> Those who have chosen to follow Christ will experience a bizarre emotional paradox while viewing the brutality. Each blow to the face, lash with the whip and nail through his flesh is simultaneously repellent *and* indisputable testimony of divine love. (Smithouser *et al.*, 2004)

To one's own group, this mixture can make patronage worthwhile: had it no violence, then watching would have less impact; were it merely repellent, then no one would watch; and were it solely for pleasure, then it would be deemed prurient and its viewers perverse. A passion's Christ suffers as sacrifice, and the faithful willingly witness this, but for what seem to them to be the best of reasons – that they may become most emotionally alive to the sacrifice made. On this logic, though both move their viewers, the erotic is fleshly where the religious is spiritual, porn entertaining and art overwhelming, one done for satisfaction and the other for love, one low and the other high – one empowering *their* group and the other empowering *ours*. The point of culture is to tell the difference.

Consider the frequency with which supporters praise Gibson for his art and its power to move them. The film shows a man tortured as his mother weeps; and stirring viewers with such footage should require little skill. In drawing compliments to its maker, aesthetic qualities of the film may matter less than the membership of the audience and their bonds with the artist.

I suggest that the status that Gibson earned with evangelicals, by visiting churches and invoking traditions, drew their flattery of his skill. Sociologically, the difference between a filmmaker's *artistry* and *exploitation* depends in part upon the aspirations of the group that favours him. Fill theatres with high-solidarity patrons who claim national importance and count the maker as one of their own, and the focus on bodies can become art not trash – overwhelming rather than titillating.[8]

Appellants countered charges of 'titillation' by citing, with disapproval, the Classification Office reference to '*A spectacle of blood and gore*' suggesting that the scene is included in the film to titillate the audience (FLBR, 2004, p. 10). Having interpreted Hastings's use of 'spectacle' to imply low culture, the Society responds:

> This is not gratuitous violence. Gratuitous violence is when you stuff violence after violence in the audience's face to titillate them. The violence is [*sic*] this film is an attempt to underscore the incredible agonising cruelty involved in this act [of crucifixion]. (quoted in New Zealand Press Association, 2004a)

One might argue that the point of any depiction of torture is to dwell on its cruelty. The distinction, should one draw it, is moral: The good group cherishes the victims sacrificed, the bad group wallows in pleasure at the sight of their pain.

In a final press release, issued once it had helped Hoyts win its appeal (which lowered the age of restriction from sixteen to fifteen), the Society argued,

> Yes, the level of violence (and consequent suffering) is high in The Passion, but it is apposite. … It is clearly not intended to, nor does it, titillate the audience, but rather overwhelms the audience with the sense of genuine self-giving sacrifice, love and forgiveness that overpowers and defeats the force of evil motivating perpetrators of violence. (SPCS, 2004b)

In this argument, one's own state of excitation at the sight of torture can elevate rather than debase, because it bears on the pain of the beloved, inspires sacrifice for and forgiveness of those around and empowers one's group to combat its foes. The noun *titillation* indicates pleasurable excitation, one often associated with porn and other prurience; and worshippers do not like to see the pleasures offered by their rituals – solidarity, faith, spiritual well-being – mistaken for those of competing groups.

Sociologically, *titillation*, like perversion, is a derogatory term for another group's pleasure, just as snuff is the other group's sacrifice, an idol the other group's god, and delusion the other group's faith. My point is neither that supporters were titillated by the film and then disavowed a pleasure that they could not admit, nor that *The Passion of the Christ* really is snuff, but rather that terms such as 'snuff' and 'titillation' are terms of distinction.[9] They tell the difference between one group and another – indirectly, by way of criticism of whatever imagery excites the other and by refusal of any comparison to their own. Polarization, the evacuation of common ground between peoples, is the point. This is how groups define themselves, scorn each other, draw their boundaries and instil the excitement of solidarity. The discussion in New Zealand of the rating of this film afforded a chance for groups to do this.

I take this story as an object lesson in the classification of film. It suggests what might have occurred in Hollywood had the MPAA challenged evangelicals and conservative Catholics, and their claims to cultural privilege, by restricting access to the film with its NC-17 rating, equating its violence to that of low genres. It might have been tantamount to branding the passion pornographic, and inflamed the very watchdogs whom CARA was founded to placate. And in doing so, the New Zealand board granted supporters of the film motive and opportunity both to claim national legitimacy and to draw their boundaries in heavy ink.

Conservative Christians in at least several nations appear to have taken the release of this film as an opportunity to show strength and celebrate their heritage. It seems unlikely in retrospect that the MPAA in the US, with its businesslike aversion to conflict with watchdogs, would have challenged evangelical Christians and conservative Catholics by assigning the film a restrictive rating. I echo Sandler's analysis of the MPAA (2007); its purpose is not to shield children or to apply standards in an even-handed way, but to protect the cartel of major studios by avoiding conflict with any groups large enough and ready to lobby for censorship. It did this by altering its classification of depictions of torture enough to avoid associating this object of subcultural ritual with either crime or generic entertainment. Censors and boards of review do not simply take movies as sets of images and sounds but must decide whether to privilege some groups over others. In that respect, the New Zealand Society's complaint is well taken – a movie is not just a movie, and its classification is affected by and signals the status of the group that supports it.

The bending of its rules by this ratings board, as it considered the demands of groups most likely to attend the release, sheds light on other boards' decisions. In a very different way, several Muslim nations likewise found themselves bending rules that govern distribution. They seem, however, to have been motivated by more than deference to Christendom.

The Fate of a Prophet

A handful of Muslim nations banned *The Passion of the Christ* altogether: Bahrain, Kuwait and Malaysia. In the latter, evangelical Christians protested, in much the same manner as churches had in New Zealand. For instance,

> The Secretary general of National Evangelical Christian Fellowship Malaysia, Reverend Wong Kim, agreed ... that a movie should not be banned unless it portrays a deplorable or inaccurate picture of a prophet, and that the government, 'should consider the sentiments and feelings of a particular religious community' that is closely tied with the film, in this case, Christians. (AsianNews.it, 2004a)

Such protests made the arguments reviewed above, on behalf of deference toward evangelical culture, but were met by the force of a longstanding ban on depictions of prophets. In Malaysia, authorities gave a bit of ground, eventually allowing screenings in churches, where, ostensibly, no one would take offence.

In Kuwait, as reported by Agence France-Presse (AFP), officials of the Sunni majority objected to the showing of the film on the grounds that its depiction of Christ's death contradicts a teaching that Christ was able to avoid crucifixion (2004). But a Shiite cleric urged that an exception be made, on the logic that 'It's a good opportunity to reveal the crimes committed by Jews against the Christ and many other (religious) prophets.'

Most other Muslim nations made that exception and allowed screenings. After a month of worldwide release, *Daily Variety* reported that Egyptian censors had passed the film uncut, even though

> few movies depicting Jesus have reached Egyptian screens. Franco Zeffirelli's 'Jesus of Nazareth' (1976) was screened for only five days in Cairo, then pulled to pacify extremist groups. Since then, all other dramatic depictions of the life of Christ have been shown on videotapes in specialized Christian libraries or in Coptic churches and cultural centers. (Fine and Osborne, 2004, p. 6)

At Al Azhar University, Cairo, a member of the Islamic Research Council (the university authority that reviews publications) claimed that it would avoid interfering with Christian culture: 'We do not accept the screening of prophets, but we cannot confiscate others' beliefs. ... We didn't review this movie because it does not concern Muslims' (quoted in Levinson, 2004).

To explain this turnabout, Mustafa Darwish, a film critic and former president of the Egypt Censorship Authority, told the *San Francisco Chronicle*'s foreign desk that 'They (the censorship authorities) think the film is anti-Semitic. That's why they are giving it such privilege' (Levinson, 2004). A professor of media and journalism at Al Azhar likewise said that, despite the university's longstanding and influential ban on depictions of prophets in movies, 'I encouraged the movie because it withholds from Jews their claims that they are innocent of the Christ's blood' (quoted in Levinson, 2004).

It is likely that widely broadcast debate in the US shaped perceptions of *The Passion of the Christ*. But it seems certain that the fact that potential audience members belonged to particular groups affected boards' decisions to bend and break longstanding rules. Cultural and nationalist conflicts can intrude even on doctrinally motivated rules of classification. The release of *The Passion of the Christ* appears to have effected as much religious disruption of censorship as any cultural event of the last few decades.

Conclusion

In each case reviewed above, the compelling factor seems to be the strength with which groups could express religious concerns as Icon sought wider distribution. Experienced regulators seemed to agree that the film posed unique challenges because it depicted a prophet, his torture, his condemnation by Jews or all three. The rules of boards around the world require restrictive ratings of such material; which is what several gave it (especially in such nations as China, Kuwait, the UK and Mexico). But religious organizations, many apparently *motivated* by the complaints of Jewish groups, were able to secure exceptions and wider release.

In most respects, this appears to be an anomalous case, as other filmmakers are unlikely to follow in Gibson's footsteps. Though a subsequent flurry of torture-focused horror releases may owe a small debt to this exception to CARA's classification of set-piece scenes of violence, lasting effects have otherwise yet to appear. Indeed, much of the fuss surrounding this release was restricted to the US, where the film made most of its profits as well as most of its headlines. I turn next to the reception of this film by American evangelicals, who made this release very much their own, as some of their spokespeople argued that film violence ought to belong to them as well.

✗ PART 3

RECEPTION

It's an honor to be chosen as a reviewer of this film. For many months, and even more strongly for the past few weeks, we've all been subjected to a propaganda campaign in the media and on the Internet, attacking *The Passion* with a variety of 'concerns' ranging from the possibly-valid to the irrelevant and outrageous. ... I believe that any reviewer of this film should state his view of the Scriptures up front, so the reader knows the worldview from which the review is written.

(Review of *The Passion of the Christ* on ChristianAnswers.net)

Worldviews rooted in group membership were major factors in post-release response to this film, as evinced by the discourse of American evangelical organizations. *The Passion of the Christ* turned out to be the most successful independently produced film ever screened in the United States. It broke opening-day box-office records and exceeded all expectations. This massive success is probably due to many factors, from horror-fan interest in the graphic bloodshed, and his American fans' loyalty to Mel Gibson, to the synergistic effect of saturation coverage that can turn a product roll-out into an event. News of sold-out houses and ecstatic responses to opening-day screenings doubtless amplified the message that people who wished to be up to date on popular culture should see this film. Hearing that so many had attended so early, and had such strong responses to the film, seems to have inspired waves of others to follow suit.

But the mammoth success of *The Passion of the Christ* in the US – one shared by such contemporary smashes as *The Lord of the Rings* (2001–3), *Spider-Man* (2002–4) and the *Harry Potter* films (2001–10) – did not translate into the sort of worldwide success enjoyed by those other movies. Most of the grandest hits of recent years do 60 to 75 per cent of their box-office business in nations outside the United States – the larger market, after all. But *The Passion of the Christ* reversed this trend and earned over 60 per cent of its box-office receipts in the US alone. That disproportionate show of support by US citizens, expressed in part by mass bookings for church groups on opening day, suggests that the most direct contributor was the initial support lent the film by stateside conservative Christian groups.

As the film appeared on screens elsewhere, its scenes of torture more than its portrayal of Jews made it controversial, and motivated most ratings boards to restrict its display. I argued above that the religious status of the film led national and industrial boards of review to bend rules and grant the film wider release. In the US, Ross Communications and Outreach, hired by Icon to sell the film, approached evangelical groups, first in Colorado Springs and then nationwide. The marketing pitch began with statements of kinship and claims of persecution, asking evangelicals to break with routine responses to media violence and help to support this release instead. I next describe those critics' replies. I begin by outlining the history of such groups within mainline and evangelical Christianity, then present their typical responses to film violence and their reaction to Icon's new film. I then contrast those statements with those of scholars who denounced it, and conclude by arguing that movie violence has been treated as an incendiary narrative tool, one that belonged to religions but which has been used by corporations in Hollywood for more secular ends. Film violence is stolen fire, and many evangelicals would like it back.

Evangelical Culture

In the early decades of a revival of US Christianity, in the late nineteenth century, 'plain folk' religion emphasized enthusiasm over the disciplined study of doctrine (quoted in Shibley, 1996, p. 13). A war with science and education isolated whole groups of orthodox Christians: Where more liberal Protestants embraced humanism and research, conservatives spurned them as threats to their faith (p. 16). Gradually, liberals became mainline Protestants, and the conservatives withdrew into an insular, mainly poor, rural, white Southern subculture, as *fundamentalists* after the Scopes trial of 1926.[10] Rejection of modernity and its mass media, in favour of rituals focused on Christ, amounted to their *culture* – all that distinguished them as a group.

After decades in retreat, however, American fundamentalists, still primarily Southern and white, were outraged by state intrusions into the local schooling of their children. Mid-century trends toward racial desegregation, science education and elimination of official prayers in classrooms inspired their return to political contest, which begat contemporary evangelicalism (Noll, 2002, p. 111). By the late 1970s, they had resumed aggressive evangelism and lobbying, and moved from merely voting for conservative candidates as private citizens to collective alignment with the Republican Party as its highly active base (Hout and Fischer, 2002).

Trends toward higher education and urban, multicultural life in the US have limited the growth of the evangelical movement, in part by shrinking the Southern, working-class population that had nurtured fundamentalism, and reducing the number of citizens who now claim religious ties (Hout and Fischer, 2002). Nevertheless, a popular sense of the US as a 'Christian nation' grew during the years prior to the release of *The Passion of the Christ*, especially among steady churchgoers (Straughn and Feld, 2010). Those years saw the US declare war on two Muslim nations in the wake of terrorist attacks; saw Christians reduce their welcome of non-Christians to community religious life; and saw evangelicals become especially suspicious of those of other faiths (Merino, 2010). The year of *The Passion of the Christ*'s release also saw evangelicals give 75 per cent of their votes to the Commander in Chief of the military campaigns (Guth *et al.*, 2006). Ironically, the separation of Church from the rest of public life and the reduction of religion's role in most public affairs have been accompanied in the US by increasing calls from conservative Christians for greater control of the public sphere (Achterberg *et al.*, 2009).

Such evangelical calls include a demand that the media consumed by their children, such as Hollywood movies, be more effectively policed. Spokespeople for their organizations have had much to say about the culture produced by other groups – little of it complimentary. By sustaining their critique of popular media, by linking mass culture to harm, watchdogs both try to better their world and mark the boundaries between their groups and others. The controversy of *The Passion of the Christ* afforded the perfect opportunity to do this.

People mostly engage with entertainment as individuals and in small groups of friends. But they can also join in solidarity through discriminating, ritual consumption. Evangelicals did precisely this during the 1988 protest against *The Last Temptation of Christ* (Lindlof, 1996) and the 1990s-era Southern Baptist boycott of the Disney Corporation (Warren, 2001), taking advantage of controversial events and using organizations to form ranks in their confrontation with Hollywood. This is the job of the media watchdogs affiliated with a number of evangelical groups, which provide some of the formal infrastructure of group bonding. The reception of *The Passion of the Christ* by Christian groups in the US provides a case in which advocates of a large subculture sought to enhance solidarity and strengthen their group, and aim for control over cultural institutions as they responded to release of a product.

To such ends, several evangelical groups maintain websites purporting to offer guides to family moviegoing, which feature enough discourse to allow examination of the more formal aspects of this subculture and its responses to controversy. By outlining patterns (moral discrimination, relatively scant interest in aesthetics, concern about the effects of film violence and calls to defend the nation's children and their subculture with political activism focused on film violence), I place their commentary on *The Passion of the Christ* in subcultural context and show how public discussion of this movie helped to alter routine assessment of movie violence.

Such sectarian film reviewing dates back to at least the mid-1930s, with the rise of Catholic black and white lists of bad and good films, and the Legion of Decency that brought pressure to bear on major studios (Walsh, 1996). By 1945, the Protestant Motion Picture Council (PMPC) had also begun to publish monthly reviews of Hollywood product in the *Christian Herald* (Linnell, 2006). Taking an ecumenical stance but distinguishing itself from the censorious Legion, *Christian Herald* reviewers celebrated the films that seemed to them to reflect good citizenship and tell Bible stories with reverence. They advised readers to make up their own minds, and celebrated the power of individuals to shop for entertainment in a free society.

This reviewing began in the postwar period when regional film boards still held sway, before the 1952 Supreme Court decision outlawed censorship. The magazine's editor wrote an open letter to Hollywood studios in 1950, threatening that,

> films are meeting with bans and boycotts galore. All this could easily snowball into something far more serious for you. … Once before, faced by the threat of political censorship, you did some very fast and quite effective house-cleaning. It looks like the time has come for another clean-up. Whether you do it yourselves, or whether you wait for public indignation to roll censorship down upon you, is up to you. (quoted in Linnell, 2006)

Such threats rang hollow after the Supreme Court outlawed censorship of studios' wares, and the evangelical emphases on civil religion and individualism sapped their remaining authority. The *Herald* ceased to publish PMPC reviews after 1966. The Catholic Council of Motion Pictures also saw its credibility vanish as Hollywood dismantled the Production Code that it had helped to build and replaced it with age-graded classification that allowed more sex and violence on screen. Though the Catholic Council had published reviews of its own for decades, bishops finally suspended its funding in 1980.

By the time of the release of *The Passion of the Christ*, however, evangelical reviewing had been given a new lease on life by conservative Protestant embrace of popular culture and the proliferation of websites during the 1990s. I base my conclusions about responses to Icon's release on my study of over a dozen sites maintained by those groups. Those movie-review archivists have used the internet to post discussions of vice and value in mass media and to review individual Hollywood releases. Most began publication and offered general statements of purpose in the late 1990s. And most have continued to provide reviews of new releases ever since. (Please see Appendix C for a fuller description of these groups and sites.)

I do not assume that this rhetoric precisely matches or fully guides responses of the tens of millions who might call themselves evangelicals or patronize those sites. These are merely organizations' statements, issuing from the most formal processes of the large and varied movement. But the post-9/11 rise of hostility toward non-Christian groups, and celebration of the US as a 'Christian nation' under cultural siege, may have intensified organizations' defences of Gibson from scholarly critique and churchgoers' support of his film.

Dangers of Media Violence

Perhaps the most vexing challenge evangelicals (organizations and moviegoers) confronted in Gibson's film was that of absorbing its gruesome violence without eroding their boundaries against *low culture* – the viscerally appealing expressions of other groups. Given their long-term practice of linking secular Hollywood's violence to real-world crime, this might have seemed challenging indeed. Film violence has drawn denunciations, boycotts, prior censorship and theatre closures for a century. Prize-fight films were banned; theatres were closed on Sundays; and boards of censorship were set up during the first decades of the twentieth century. Most new visual media arouse concern that intense entertainment will overwhelm the better judgments of children with flattering depictions of mischief (Starker, 1989).

Responses to such new media, or to new uses of them, are not uniform but are shaped by relations between organizations, including those of religious audiences. In his history of responses to passion plays on stage and on screen, historian Charles Musser notes that initial agreements, between Protestant groups keen to influence mass culture and filmmakers anxious to do business unfettered, broke down. And when they did, concerns about the effects of mass media arose:

> the interests of showmen and evangelists were too divergent for peace to last for long. As cinema became a form of mass entertainment with the proliferation of specialized motion picture theaters after 1906, evangelical Christians quickly began to see these nickelodeons as 'schools for crime'. (1996, p. 66)

Contemporary activism follows this pattern, as I next show with a review of evangelical guidance for moviegoers.

During the run-up to the release of *The Passion of the Christ*, a reviewer critiquing *The Texas Chainsaw Massacre* (1974) for Focus on the Family's *Plugged In* complained of R ratings for action and horror films that

> easily deserved NC-17 ratings, so as to keep them out of mainstream theaters and out of the hands (minds) of teens and children. But the MPAA callously slapped both with an R. Did anyone on the ratings board actually *see* them?

Violence presented without obvious justification earns the harshest disparagement. *Preview* warns that,

> Sadistic and gratuitous violence can desensitize viewers to violence and even encourage them to act out what they see on the screen. In a time when violent crime is a major concern in this country, the last thing we need is for movies to encourage it. (Evans, 1996b)

In line with a much larger crusade against media violence,[11] reviewers argue that the worst of the films can drive children to crime. Of the 1994 Hollywood release *Natural Born Killers*, one writes,

The film is as offensive and vulgar as the crimes [Oliver Stone]'s criticizing, glamorizing every kind of nasty killing and sexual assault. ... Disgusting and disturbing, *Natural Born Killers* is, in the words of one of its characters, 'Bad! Bad! Bad!' It is truly an abomination. (*Preview*)

And, in a review that barely comments upon the substance of the movie, another critic raising the spectre of government control, warns that

Hollywood stands accused of recklessly celebrating violence – including acts which have led to the corruption of teens and the victimization of innocent people. The evidence is overwhelming. But can filmmakers really be held liable for damage caused by their products? Can the entertainment industry be compared to a careless auto manufacturer or an irresponsible pharmaceutical firm? Some legal experts believe so, and hope that their objections to voyeuristic cinematic slaughter are sustained. (*Plugged In*)

Reviewers urge that we use the government to shield children, neighbours and ourselves from the violence encouraged by movies that use it for anything but clear moral instruction on behalf of righteous groups. Publishing organs of these conservative Christian groups have cited media-effects research and networked with politicians as they develop family-friendly policies and urge regulation. In his study of twentieth-century Catholic activism in Hollywood, Walsh (1996) observes that the evangelical site *MovieGuide* urges restrictive policies remarkably similar to those of the Production Code of decades before. (By the 1990s, evangelicals had become the more censorious, and Catholics had assumed the contrary position of treating moviegoing as a matter of individual conscience (1996, p. 331)).

Ready for battle, evangelical authors rattle sabres with mentions of their political connections. One author for a website studied here states that,

Al Gore's office recently called our ministry asking for more information on what we do and requesting copies of our movie and TV review publications. To a large extent, the deterioration in movies and TV has come about by a strong shift to degenerate and ungodly characters, and a trend away from characters with wholesome life styles. (Evans, 1996b)

They worry that screen violence can deprave children if used to tell the wrong stories, by the wrong people, for the wrong reasons; and these websites sound alarms. Writes one, "'There should be no more debate about this issue," said Eric Hotmire, [Republican Senator] Brownback spokesman. "Violent entertainment affects children in a negative way"' (Winn, 2000). And such writers refer not merely to harm that may come to the families of others, but to their own fears of 'the powerful negative influence movies exert on their impressionable children' (Rolfe, 2004).

Writes another,

many studies show decisively that the behavior of movie and TV viewers is affected by what they see on the screen. I am convinced that if any Christian, either youth or adult, continues to feed on the many degenerate movies of today, this will eventually damage his or her moral and spiritual life. So, what can we Christians do to combat this threat? (Evans, 1996a)

What they can do, to protect youth of their own, is call upon Hollywood not to produce immoral violence and their children not to watch it. However, this is not to say that all media violence strikes these reviewers as immoral.

Uses of Media Violence

Evangelical reviews distinguish between functions of screen bloodshed, whether it be enlisted amorally to increase profit or for valid goals, such as honouring fallen soldiers or bringing souls to Christ. The Childcare Action Project states its moral criterion for violence: 'If a scene is violent, the CAP model notes it as such whether "justified" by actual events or not.' Reviewers privilege movies in which the central characters, be they abused martyrs or righteous scourges, are the recognizable heroes of Western-nationalist or Biblical stories: *Saving Private Ryan* and Gibson's own *Braveheart*, and Christian-authored allegories such as *The Lord of the Rings* and *The Chronicles of Narnia* (2005–8). Where the former lay claims to historical authenticity, the latter appear to reviewers to be grounded in more spiritual truths. To evangelical critics, either will do.

Consider the reviews of 1998's *Saving Private Ryan*, which became a frequently cited precedent in debates over violence in *The Passion of the Christ*:

> There is no movie that can compare, no other feeling on Earth that will shock you as this movie does. That is, unless you actually fought in the war. It is disturbing, it is ferocious, it is unyielding, it is absolute hell on Earth. And, in your mind, you'll swear up and down that it's real. ... The final battle is the closest you will ever get to fighting a war. You feel like taking shelter behind the chair in front of you.

This reviewer, working for Christian Answers, means all of that in a good way. Christian Critic also lauds the depiction of loyalties to higher callings: '*Saving Private Ryan* does not sanitize that brutality for us. It fully displays the unmistakable ugliness of war at the same time exalting the courage and dedication to duty of the men that lived through it (or died trying).' Movie Reporter describes it as, 'A powerful film that has led to a renewed interest in the sacrifices made during WW2.' Film violence can garner such praise when it is rooted in a national heritage, celebrates a nation's heroes and pays close attention to sacrifice for God and country.

However, the force of film violence can also intrude; and other sites (CAP, *Plugged In* and *Preview*) remain unconvinced of the value of the bloodshed, even when used to illustrate such a story. The violence strikes some as overdone, 'gratuitous'; and such instances of shocking gore seem to hamper the film's ability to convey truths. Writes *MovieGuide*,

SAVING PRIVATE RYAN, contains a mild moral worldview with positive references to God and some Christian elements. It also dilutes the Christianity and religious beliefs of the real American soldiers in that conflict, and its characters and final climax fail to be completely engrossing.

Such movies put reviewers in a difficult position: able to appreciate themes of martial courage, devout faith and final sacrifice, as well as the central position of national heroes; but often recoiling from the force with which such movies strike their viewers.

Consider reviews of Mel Gibson's 1995 war movie *Braveheart* (set during medieval Scotland's struggle for independence). They note with approval its factual basis and patriotic lessons, even as they wish for less carnage on screen:[12]

Wallace reflects a strong religious belief as he has a priest bless his marriage and his troops before battles, and he prays for strength before he is tortured. One of his followers often talks to God aloud … . Unfortunately, *Braveheart*'s authentic battle scenes demand a brave stomach. (*Preview*)

At its core lies a fundamental life-and-death struggle for what so many 21st-century Americans take for granted … life, liberty and the pursuit of happiness. … Leaving a bit more to the imagination would have made *Braveheart* a more accessible entertainment without diminishing its inherently powerful messages. (*Plugged In*)

As a Christian-themed war film rather than a passion depicting the most godly sacrifice, a film such as *Braveheart* earns qualified support.

Though it earned fewer Hollywood awards than *Braveheart, The Passion of the Christ* met with greater acclaim from these reviewers. Gibson's stardom (a symbol of the mass culture that they wish to alter), Christian sincerity and deference to their moral authority appear to have combined to endear him to evangelicals, whose reviewers responded in kind: 'A clever fellow indeed, this Mel Gibson. Welcome to the Bride, my brother in Christ' (Childcare Action Project review). The warmth of this reception extended to a sanctioning of the violence of his film, by distinguishing it from that of any other films.

This distinction appears to rest both on the film's non-fiction status and on its depiction of the core sacrifice of their own group's history – that of their nation (as in *Saving Private Ryan*), their larger culture (Western, as in the case of *Braveheart*) or of the followers of their faith. The response to the violence on screen transformed accordingly:

> Even I, one who has seen in film every imaginable gore, shuddered in shame (shame for my sins that put Jesus in this situation) and looked away as the Roman whipmaster, with glee on his face, embedded the metal bits at the ends of the scourge cords into our Lord then yanked them out ... and pieces of our Lord with them. Brutally. Viciously. Sadistically. Yes, this movie is that violent. Beyond the capacity of words to tell. (CAP)

Such reaction to *The Passion of the Christ* suggests that intense violence, correctly used, can transcend its status as poison to become redemptive. Says the head of a PR firm that specializes in marketing movies to faith-based communities, 'It's beautiful and tragic. For Christians, it's like watching a family member being beaten up for two hours. People will be deeply moved' (Smith, 2003).

This response contrasts with those of scholars and critics who move through different professional and personal circles. I review those rejections of this film's violence before returning to evangelical defences of it. As before the film's release, each group was able to use discussion of *The Passion of the Christ* to attack the other's worldview.

The Scholars and Violence

Scholars have been nearly unanimous in their failure to applaud this film, pairing repudiation of its morals with warnings of its effects and opposition to the groups that supported its release. Journals devoted whole issues to denunciations (e.g., *Journal of Literary Studies* vol. 21 no. 2, 2005); and some authors have written with unabashed scorn (e.g., Márquez, 2006; Thistlethwaite, 2004, 2009). Some psychoanalyzed Gibson, with colourful but unlikely stories of masochism and even deprogramming (Heschel, 2006, p. 102; Rubenstein, 2006, p. 113).[13] Some have levelled the charge of sexual titillation that so offended the New Zealand protestors (Heschel, 2006, p. 103; Enders, 2006, p. 188). Many condemned the violence on theological grounds. For instance, Miller argues that the logic of substitutionary atonement (which holds that, with His passion, Jesus paid the debts that humans owe to God for having sinned so much) elides aspects of Christ's life that Bible scholars celebrate as salvific: his incarnation, teachings, resurrection and fealty to the kingdom of God under threat of death (2006, pp. 41–3).

Other scholars have measured the damage done; Levine (2004, p. 209) and Fredriksen (2006, p. 97) recount the anti-Semitic graffiti, vandalism and 'hate crimes' that trailed the film's release. Where evangelical reviewers had for years warned of the threat of copycat violence in the wake of films such as *Natural Born Killers* and *Fight Club* (1999), a few scholars sounded a comparable alarm about *The Passion of the Christ*.

Leon Wieseltier, the literary editor of the *New Republic* who had published one of Fredriksen's critiques of Gibson, responded to the film with three pages of warning and invective, later reprinted in the principal scholarly collection on the film (Burnham, 2004). Wieseltier wrote of perceiving a 'lurid style', 'a repulsive masochistic fantasy', and 'contempt for the moral sensitivities of people'. He urged that 'children must be protected from it' (2004, p. 19). Writing like a scholar of religion, he also offered few concessions to the orthodox: 'Religious belief may actually interfere with a lucid analysis of religious life' (p. 20), and 'the Gospels are not clear and reliable historical documents' (p. 21). The occasion of the film's release provided many who preserve such ties (liberal and academic journals, maintained by trained scholars and their peers from elite universities) a chance to distance themselves from the literalists outside their academies.

I have already reviewed the predictions of anti-Semitic violence that scholars made after reading the script. So pitched did the rhetoric become that a few wrote as though they had lost all track of time and money. For example: 'It is, in fact, the highest grossing R-rated movie in the history of film. The flogging of Jesus by the Romans goes on for fully 40 minutes. It is truly the most violent film I have ever seen' (Thistlethwaite, 2009). (In fact, the flogging lasts about ten minutes; and the inflation-adjusted grosses of *The Passion of the Christ* are dwarfed by those of such R-rated fare as *The Godfather* (1972) or *Beverly Hills Cop* (1984).) Such exaggeration fits a pattern in which aggressive activity among a community of foes not only increases one's sense of threat but can lead to imputations of unreason (as with Gibson's assertion of a link between scholarship and perversion, quoted in Part 1). The same author concludes with a denial that conservative theology has any basis in gospel:

> The message of the movie, and a message of a lot of conservative Christian theology, is that severe pain and suffering are not foreign to Christian faith, but central. Of course, this is an interpretation of Jesus' life, death and resurrection that I reject. It is also an interpretation that I believe has done a lot of harm through the centuries. I think it is impossible, yes, *impossible*, if you read the Gospels, to make the case that God wanted Jesus tortured for the sins of humanity. (Thistlethwaite, 2009)

In this way, at least a few scholars used critique of the film to dismiss the most fundamental values of competing professions and subcultures.

Few scholars join crusades against media violence; and those who have do not agree on its effects. But one of the more ambitious scholarly initiatives was telling in its opposition to conservativism in general and fundamentalism in particular. Communication scholar George Gerbner organized his peers against media violence because he thought that it made people less liberal. As the *Atlantic* describes his view,

> The sheer quantity of violence on television encourages the idea that aggressive behavior is normal. Viewers become desensitized. The mind, as Gerbner puts it, becomes 'militarized.' ... we become fearful and anxious – and more willing to depend on authorities, strong measures, gated communities, and other proto-police-state accouterments. ... 'Punitive and vindictive action against dark forces in a mean world is made to look appealing, especially when presented as quick, decisive, and enhancing our sense of control and security'. (Stossel 1997, p. 91)

Gerbner and his liberal colleagues called for democratic control of Hollywood storytelling, in order to save their nation from repression:

> Fundamentalists have pre-empted the cultural issue. ... The culture wars are heating up, and we need a liberating alternative to stop fundamentalists from expropriating the issue and taking it in a repressive direction. (quoted in Stossel, 1997, p. 102)

Scholars have taken aim at violence not just as conservative evangelicals have, but in opposition to them. Whatever the overlaps between these large groups, they fade from view as battle lines form. Culture is what divides us from them (however provisional the 'us' and the 'them' might be). For many scholars, *bad* violence, and *repressive* approaches to regulating Hollywood, are those that appeal to conservative Christians.

Redemption through Media Violence

While so many scholars treated it as lunatic porn, the makers of *The Passion of the Christ* embraced religious groups and received warm welcome in return. Icon producer McEveety acknowledges (on the DVD commentary released in 2007) that many avoided *The Passion of the Christ* for fear of its graphic bloodshed. The film offers 'one intense moment after the next' and evoked strong responses from audiences. But, in his account of extensive screenings during post-production, he notes that 'real Christians … felt empowered by this and felt that we'd done the right job'.

Indeed, I have found no concern expressed by evangelical critics that *The Passion of the Christ* would do worse than frighten small children or drive the weak of stomach away. None worried that the images of soldiers and Jews tormenting Christ would inspire viewers to commit copycat crimes, or that the depiction would inflame anti-Semitic passions. In its review, Dove opines, 'I suspect that many non-Christians will, at the very least, be impacted by the vivid portrayal of an innocent man who was mercilessly beaten and unfairly executed because of those who either hated or feared him.' Defences of the film by other evangelicals include: 'I can't imagine anyone finding pleasure, sexual or otherwise, in Gibson's depiction of Christ's agony any more than I can imagine being inspired by it to commit violence. It's just horrifying' (Sobran, 2004). These reviewers argued that good Christians, however they may feel about violence in other films, should try and appreciate the truth that this one conveys.

First, critics excused the film's graphic nature by noting its need of such imagery, in service of the world's most important story, for audiences jaded by decades of cinema: '[T]echniques of extreme graphic violence have been used in films of all types, from war movies with a message of self-sacrifice to ridiculous horror and horror-comedy flicks. Moviegoing audiences are desensitized …' (Christian Answers). The solution proposed to counter this jadedness of the audience is a graphic 'realism'.

In his study of evangelical responses, Prince (2006) argues that such reviewers complimented filmmakers for their 'realism' not because the film showed actual violence as one might see it with no mediation, but instead because the amplitude of the style exceeded that of anything they had ever seen: torture took up much of the running time, soundtrack and space on screen, where in other passion films such violence appears small, makes little noise and vanishes fast. Greater focus on the taboo events that most films elide may strike viewers as 'realistic', while viewers in groups hostile to the film may see the opposite quality, as in the case of this scholar's review:

> We are talking about an action flick here. Aficionados of the genre, and of Gibson's stellar contributions to it, know that realism is not one of its (or his) hallmarks. Actors routinely 'bleed' in visually striking, medically remarkable ways, thanks to the makeup artist's skill. (Fredriksen, 2004, p. 60)

Fellow scholar Witherington III likewise argues that, 'Realistically, Jesus should never have even survived that onslaught, much less been able to carry or help carry an extra-large, entire cross all the way to Golgotha' (2004, p. 88). Group membership shaped perceptions of realism, such that evangelicals saw more where scholars sensed less. As supporters of the film, evangelical critics allowed that a 'realistic' level of graphic violence, one that exceeded Hollywood standards, could hold the attention of viewers.

The second step in the justification of the film's violence involves a reminder of theological priorities: 'Jesus' ESSENTIAL role was not that of a Teacher, but of a Savior. ... The essence of this story is Jesus' sacrifice – the BLOOD that so many of our songs sing about' (Christian Answers). These evangelical understandings of Christianity focus on the mystery of the cross, the ransom paid for human souls in the form of the blood of Christ.

I do not mean to suggest that evangelical Christians were quick to accept unprecedented depictions of torture. Preview audiences told Gibson that those scenes ran too long (Boyer, 2003; Munoz, 2004); and he appears to have trimmed them in compromise (a process that he would extend into preparation of the 'Recut' release in 2005, as I discuss in the conclusion to this book). Upon release, some Christian reviewers found the gore excessive and urged Protestant discussion over Catholic iconography (e.g., Overstreet, 2004; Sterritt, 2004). Nevertheless, when push came to shove after months of debate, and leaders urged followers to show their support, reviewers made a point of suspending normal judgments:

> There have been complaints that the film is too violent – too gory – too bloody. … It is not easy to watch – especially if you love God and His son. But it is true to fact. His actual 'trial' and execution were also too violent, too bloody and too gory. (Christian Critic)

> According to *Preview*'s standards, the violence would earn this film a negative acceptability rating, but if there was ever a place where violence is appropriate, or acceptable, this is it (*Preview*).

> Based on Dove's ratings criteria, we are unable to award the Family Approved Seal. People have often speculated that if a movie of these stirring events was ever made graphically and truthfully, it would have to be R-rated. I personally believe that this time the 'R' should stand for 'Redemptive'. (Dove)

And critics measured goodness of the footage by its ennobling effects. Wrote a patron of Christian Answers (in terms representative of the posts of many others on that site),

> I watched as my Lord and Saviour was scourged, beaten, spat upon, and crucified for me. Tears rolled down my cheeks in rivers. … I am closer to Jesus now after witnessing his sacrifice for me in it's [*sic*] full horror and brutality.

A contributor to Crosswalk commented:

> The beatings and torture are savage – more so than anything I have ever seen onscreen. … At the very least, parents should see this film

themselves before deciding whether to allow their children to attend. The rest of us, however, should all see 'The Passion' every year, for the rest of our lives – lest we take it for granted, lest we forget.

Beyond defending this exception to their general condemnation of vivid bloodshed on screen, reviewers also charged the film's harshest critics with hypocrisy, and demonstrated again the force of group membership on debate over controversial film. For instance, the Christian Answers review of *The Passion of the Christ* scoffed at warnings of copycat violence:

> So many of the voiced objections betray a double standard. This film is being judged by a different set of rules than any other. And the people who always proclaim that movies are just entertainment and don't really change behavior or beliefs – where are those people now? I don't hear them. The silence is deafening.

Focus on the Family head Dobson (2004) offered a similar view, of a critic who objected to this depiction of torture:

> Isn't it telling that in every other situation – with the exception of this movie – [one of the critics of *The Passion of the Christ*] has sat silent as Hollywood churned out one sultry, sadistic and crude film after the other?

To at least some evangelical reviewers, the condemnation of Gibson's film, which seemed to emanate from secular and scholarly circles, suggested bad faith. They responded with a charge of hypocritical contradiction.

From any group's vantage, the statements of another may seem foreign enough in logic to betray a double standard or lack coherence. So might the statements of scholars and secular critics strike evangelical reviewers. Like many ratings boards, professional critics had noticed that *The Passion of the Christ* featured much longer scenes of torture than any R-rated film ever had before; and they had drawn a distinction according to professional norms. To some of these evangelical reviewers, however, this distinction seemed strained – a double standard. Those reviewers assessed the legitimacy of the film's violence in the same way they had that of its realism, artistic value and lack of titillating or criminogenic effect. They gauged these in terms of the depiction of genuine sacrifice for a group of high moral status enjoying national legitimacy. On this basis, they judged the violence to be educative and ennobling. They appear to have seen little sense in critical judgments to the contrary and took advantage of the opportunity to express social distance with their charge of double standards.

Mocked by liberal pundits and scholars as anti-Semites, some evangelical reviewers also joined filmmakers in reversing those claims of victimhood. Scholars had expressed fears that the film might provoke anti-Semitic violence, just as sectarian critics have long worried about the effects of certain Hollywood genres on their children. Some evangelicals saw these imputations of potential ill effect as expressions not only of self-serving double standards but of outright hostility toward Christianity.

> [T]he idea of a movie that accurately portrays the death and resurrection of Christ and that 'has the power to evangelize' is more than certain members of the liberal media establishment can stomach … [T]he movie – and Mel Gibson himself – have been mercilessly dogged by liberal commentators hurling unfair criticism and baseless allegations [that the movie could] be a catalyst for renewed outbreaks of anti-Jewish sentiment around the world. (Dobson, 2004)

By interpreting critique of the film as a slight on conservative Christendom, reviewers reinforced a sense of embattled identity. The organization *See The Passion.com* posted an internet petition declaring Christian support of the film, with the argument that, 'This battle has become bigger than Mel Gibson, and even bigger than this movie itself. It is a defining moment in the Culture War for the future of our country, our civilization and the world' (Women Influencing the Nation, 2004). The petition itself observed that, 'We know that the enemies of Christian civilization – who are identifying themselves for all to see by announcing themselves as the enemies of this movie project – will maneuver till the end to block this movie' (Women Influencing the Nation, 2004).

Such statements, the most radical in this supportive discourse, suggest larger stakes behind some of the enthusiasm for this film: defence of community, and definition of it through imputations of both incoherence ('double standard') and hostility ('Culture War') to outsiders ('liberal[s]'). The Southern Baptist Convention president claimed that the movie's success was 'a providence from God, that in the middle of an international war on terrorism, in the midst of a cultural and domestic war for the family, God raises up a standard' (quoted in Gates, 2004, p. 50). The marketing and reviewing of this film lent themselves to wartime solidarity and the drawing of the starkest boundaries. 'This was a chance to carry your placard for Jesus, and say to everyone, "This is our story. We want you to understand and appreciate our story"' (quoted in Caldwell, 2004, p. 224). Christian Smith, a long-time scholar of Christianity, has referred to American evangelicals as 'embattled' though engaged with their culture (Smith and Emerson, 1998). 'Evangelicals have a side that really craves respect, and this was something they could feel they're a part of' (quoted in Caldwell, 2004, p. 223).

On the accounts of these internet reviews, some bouts of movie violence alienate us from God and humankind, potentially causing crime, while others draw people together. For them, good standing as (evangelical) group members – *culture*, in a word – requires a moral certainty about which violence has which effects. Violence entailing a champion's sacrifice on behalf of a group can improve its audience. That which does not involve such sacrifice seems like the cheapest of thrills and can engender destruction. Such reviewing asks parents to choose movies that either use violence sparingly or use it to teach values of self-sacrifice to family, government and God. These reviews do what culture does – distinguish one's group from others. In this sense, evangelical critics took the debate over the release as a chance to reclaim what they felt had been stolen.

Stolen Fire

The industrialization of religious culture created a mass media able to serve secular goals. This has led to a turf war, in which many Christians fight to regain control over popular storytelling. The usurpation by secular merchants has often been insidious, as when exhibitors harnessed a silent passion film to 'inscribe moving pictures into the context of "the sacred"' in 1907 (Grieveson, 2004, p. 85), and when the film industry's trade press linked the uplifting functions of cinema to those of the Church over the next few years (pp. 86–7). By such means, filmmakers inserted themselves between religious authorities and the mass storytelling that they felt they ought to govern.

Clerics once enjoyed more control. Ancient culture teemed with gods offended, peoples slaughtered, heroes martyred and sinners punished – in stories told by religious groups to affirm the sacred and bolster members' spiritual commitment. Staging passion plays as the word of God rather than as fiction, evangelists could use violence in aid of potent rituals, calling participants to bow before real powers in legitimate groups rather than to cheer fiction in deviant ones. Those who screen such films to potential converts report sudden and profound responses (Eshleman, 2002); and so may passion films move believers, change lives and keep faith groups strong.

But clerics and evangelists have found themselves competing, with similar tools and images, with less demanding organizations for loyalty. Mass media have featured big-selling stories composed for corporate profit, which employ stirring images of combat between heroes and villains, blood sacrifice and other violence, but remove them from ritual contexts and steal the force of sectarian myth. Where many religious groups challenge people to give their lives to God, tithe to organizations and volunteer for service, entertainers ask merely that customers sit through commercials or buy tickets for thrills. As Musser (1996) puts it, moviemaking

> entrepreneurs exploited religious subject[s] for their own commercial
> purposes, ultimately assimilating them into the emerging culture of mass

amusements. In the process, they gradually wrested greater control over the construction of these images and narratives, even as the clergy who made or showed them sought to use them to evangelize the masses. (pp. 63–4)

In this sense, media violence is stolen fire, thieved by consumer capitalists from clerics who unite groups in faith, and engaged to sell trivia to shoppers instead.

With this in mind, it seems ironic that so many critics accused Gibson of trading in the imagery of action and horror as he constructed his film. Though mass media have turned bloodshed into secular fun, after all, that very imagery belonged once to sects. I therefore urge that we extend Musser's argument beyond the substance of passion plays and apply it to their violence as well. The story of the passion is bloody, featuring acts of suicide, torture, mutilation and execution. The violence of such drama, loosed from its ritual context and co-opted to enliven films about horror or crime, strikes evangelical reviewers as tasteless and sinful. Writers declare most media violence harmful, even in the absence of correlations between the circulation of fiction and trends in violent crime. One ought not to resort to incendiary images merely to amuse, these reviews teach their readers; and one should never use them to subvert shared morals or mock the godly. Movie violence burns too easily into our brains, they claim; we ought to enlist it only to illustrate the stories of heroes whose bloodshed founded our groups.

Sociologically, *low culture* consists of viscerally compelling imagery that celebrates the values of another, less righteous group. Feature-film mayhem does not so much abandon the moral discourse of religion as compete with it, appealing to different groups, screened for different reasons. In the case of Hollywood product, it inspires people to make smaller and more individual offerings than those called for by religious groups. The result of this competition seems to be a turf war, for which evangelical organizations have sounded calls to arms and threatened censorship. At the extremes, spokespeople for some of these groups demand that media violence be returned and largely restricted to their own traditions. For them, media violence is sacred and can be dangerous when exploited by others. When used for good (for their groups), they argue, screen mayhem teaches noble truths; when used otherwise, it damages the mind.

Secular feature films partake of such similar imagery, narratives and visceral force that they seem to threaten not so much the *themes* or *morals* of religious mythology, as the *monopoly* of religious groups on it. Hollywood might appear to have challenged both religious and state legitimacy with a claim of its own to incendiary myth. The release of *The Passion of the Christ* gave evangelical critics a reason to articulate the morals of movie violence, commend loyalty to their groups and denounce the work of others. To be such a critic is to invoke movie violence to win souls for the nation and bring them back to Christ; to tell the difference between us and them; and to make the critical distinction between godly passion and stolen fire.

✖ PART 4

PLOTTING

Having reviewed the marketing, rating and reception of *The Passion of the Christ*, I devote the rest of this book to the film itself, a Hollywood movie with a story to tell and effects to procure on its viewers. I first show how filmmakers adapted their sources and framed the story. In doing so, they observed Hollywood-style character-driven plotting but selectively omitted some motivations. These patterns help explain how the film satisfied evangelical groups but drew scorn from others.

The filmmakers followed Hollywood conventions by casting recognized actors in key, sympathetic roles (Jesus and Magdalen). They worked to keep the story clear by endowing most characters with one or two easily recognized traits and (reluctantly) subtitling dialogue that states motivation. Scenarists also cleaved to conventional structure, breaking their film into four acts[14] which provide emphasis on regretful but powerless witnesses to the condemnation of Christ: Judas, Pilate and Simon. Though the story introduces three loyal supporters (Mary, Magdalen and John) early and sticks with them throughout, it pivots on the movements of the three men whose interventions fail to ease the Christ's pain. I do not mean that Jesus and Mary, who have the most time on screen, are not central to the story. I mean merely that they have no *character arcs*, in Hollywood parlance. Any internal shifts that they undergo seem slight in comparison to the obvious struggles of Judas and Pilate, and to the change in Simon's feelings as he helps to carry the cross. To the extent that Hollywood plotting is structured by protagonists' struggles to meet changing goals, then the *plot* of this film belongs to these three male onlookers.[15] By focusing attention in this way, the writers may have made it easier for a viewer to feel like a sympathetic but guilty party: one may love the suffering Christ but be unable to end the pain he endures, benefiting from it as a sinner saved by grace. We each bear guilt but may gain forgiveness, the story as plotted goes.

The other major characters on screen are the Judean priests and guards, Roman officers and soldiers who most immediately persecute Jesus. The screenwriters' largest departure from convention was to leave both the plans of God and the malice of those tormentors largely unexplained (undermotivated, in screenwriter parlance). By doing this, I argue below, they appear to have helped polarize audiences, inviting fundamentalists to join in worship while alienating many of those less invested in Gibson's suspicions of Jews and theology of substitutionary atonement (by which the suffering of Jesus paid the debts that humans owe to God for having sinned so much).

The following discussions detail these narrative strategies and recount the responses of critics and friends of the film.

Narrative Structure

The film consists of four large sequences that operate as the dramatic acts of classical narrative. Such arcs lend emphasis to elements of the story by highlighting them at transitional points, which clarify the progress of central protagonists toward clearly indicated goals (Thompson, 1999). This structure provides, via regular breaks in the action and restatements of protagonists' progress, narrative clarity to a film that otherwise depends upon prior education in the gospel story.

Act One opens with sixteen minutes of blue-lit night in the Garden of Gethsemane and ends with Judas' horror at the beating of Christ. A twenty-minute trial then unfolds in town and temple, lit in warmer tones of amber and brown. It features Judas' attempt to gain the release of Christ and ends with his suicide at dawn. In this way, Act One uses film style to mark off its segments, which end on the horror of Judas at the results of his actions. Scenarist Fitzgerald says that the original idea for the script was that, 'Often, in the course of these fifteen hours, it was going to be the people around our Lord, not what was happening to him, that was going to be controlling the story' (Shepherd et al., 2004). And indeed this opening act, with its sequence-

Screen capture: Act One ends with a conclusive response
to having betrayed one's saviour.

ending pauses on Judas, offers signs that the story's progress will hinge on
those who at first aid but then try to prevent the execution. As is typical of
a dramatic set-up, the opening of the film introduces main characters and a
dramatic question: What becomes of an attempt to stop the persecution by
one who is partly to blame?

After a morbid pause over the protagonist's corpse, the film serves
notice of the transition to Act Two by revealing a new location and a new
protagonist. A second trial occurs inside the Roman fort before the governor

Screen capture: Pilate ends Act Two in frustration
at having to order Jesus' crucifixion.

Pilate. Like Judas, Pilate evolves the goal of freeing Jesus; but he gradually condemns him anyway. As the official exposition of the film puts it, this is a major turning point: 'when Pilate pronounces his verdict, it's the real beginning of Christ's execution' (Bartunek, 2005, p. 105). Where Judas ended the first act in despair, Pilate finishes the second in frustration at feeling constrained to order the killing.

Act Three establishes another new setting, on the road through Jerusalem. As Christ weakens, soldiers force Judean passerby Simon to assist. The act ends as these two look to Golgotha where Jesus must die. Simon notes that the condemned man is 'almost done'. He has become the third onlooker who facilitates the torture while sympathizing with Christ.

Hollywood melodrama typically ends its third acts on dark notes (kidnappings, threats and demoralizing defeats are common), establishing darkness-before-dawn moments of crisis to prime viewers for final scenes. Indeed, this film nears the end of its third act on a note that will seem dark indeed to those who dread the coming death. Christ looks toward Golgotha, where agony awaits; and the closest bystander, though sympathetic, can do no more than to note the imminence of that end. Like Judas and Pilate before him, Simon is sensitive to injustice but unable to stop it.

Screen capture: Simon ends Act Three on a note of foreboding, as he and Jesus look upon the killing ground.[16]

By this point, the plotting has taught the same lesson about powerless sympathy three times, but also varied it by featuring witnesses in different positions to help: Judas the maddened traitor, Pilate the weakened ruler and Simon the stranger forced to carry the cross. At this climactic moment, Gibson also provides an interlude of sorts, in part because preview audiences requested more of Christ's teachings to leaven scenes of his pain. And so, reshoots delivered brief moments of the sermon on the mount at the end of Act Three, in which Christ preaches forgiveness of those who betray and fail him.

Gibson reports that, by the time of these sermon-on-the-mount reshoots, after having been forced to defend the film against charges of anti-Semitism, he could identify all the more with the Christ who bears scorn yet forgives the Jews. He said that it made sense, at the time, to show Jesus preaching love for one's enemies, as Gibson tried to love his own. In this way, the controversies reviewed above appear to have affected editing decisions.

Simon's story having ended, the point of crisis being reached and the forgiveness of protagonists affirmed by the interlude, all that remains in Act Four is to belabour Christ's death and others' responses. The act opens with a striking musical cue and a wide shot of the march up to the final new setting, on Golgotha. Simon departs in despair and soldiers carry out the execution. After Jesus dies on that hill, a storm expresses God's grief; and cries of anguish suggest priests' and the devil's defeats. After a deposition, Christ rises to martial drums.

This plot structure is interesting not only for what it reveals about the filmmakers' interests in substitutionary atonement, but also for how it fits into a century of Jesus films made in Hollywood. I turn next to that history, to suggest how the plot and degrees of overt character motivation affected response to the film.

Character Focus

In his history of passion plays, Musser (1996) shows that evangelical Protestants crusaded to restrict early depictions of Christ on screen. It seemed disrespectful, to them, that filmmakers would make God an animated phantom in a medium devoted to thrills. Partly bowing to such pressure, early depicters of Christ mimicked the more staid 'magic lantern' slideshows that toured the nation as lectures for reverent viewers. Filmmakers copied those lectures by staging gospels as series of tableaux rather than as plot- and character-driven stories. They avoided the novelistic focus on Christ as a protagonist with both clear motivation and a character arc that would suggest a complex psychology. Likewise, American writers and publishers avoided centring their Biblical fiction on Christ because this might seem to challenge the Bible's authority and thereby risk sacrilege. Successful examples of works managing to avoid the situating of Christ as protagonist included Lew Wallace's 1880 bestseller *Ben-Hur: A Tale of Christ*, which focused instead on a bystander to the passion and eventual recruit to Christian worship.

The first full-length narrative treatment of Jesus on screen was produced by one of Hollywood's greatest showmen, once his career had been established and he could afford to run such a risk. As Richard Maltby (1990) documents, Cecil B. DeMille aimed to produce a blockbuster Christ and spared little expense on his 1927 silent. Though the film was intensively publicized to Protestant groups (much as *The Greatest Story Ever Told* in 1965 and *The Passion of the Christ* after yet another four decades would be), the release drew protests against the film's anti-Semitism and appears to have soured Hollywood on similar ventures for decades to come (Cole, 1960). (I discuss the scandal in Part 5.)

When major studios returned to the gospels, they focused on followers and their battles with Rome rather than on the conflict between Christ and his persecutors. With such adaptations of popular novels as *The Robe* (1953) and *Ben-Hur* (1959), Hollywood scored hits that seemed to satisfy the desire for animated gospel without offending piety. I suggest that they did this in part by avoiding extended focus on the two touchiest topics in the passion story: the motivations of Christ and those of the Judean priests who call for his death.

By keeping their distance from Christ, these mid-century blockbusters avoided presentation of an actor pretending to be God and rendering a complex inner life in a story structured by his character arc. That psychological staple of Hollywood storytelling makes for compelling narrative and intense involvement but struck many as inappropriate to the depiction of God. The dramatic tensions and development adopted by classical Hollywood storytelling to engage viewers were displaced onto the onlookers instead, who begin ignorant of Christ's mission but wind up in his thrall.

Subsequent experiments in the full-length presentations of Jesus as *King of Kings* (1961) and *The Greatest Story Ever Told* also kept their distance from the inner life of Christ, but in another way that met with less success. In those presentations, Jesus is a changeless stalwart with no obvious inner life. Those depictions struck many as too external, alienating and inert for extended focus in Hollywood's character-driven storytelling, and bored rather than outraged audiences. The releases disappointed their producers (indeed, the 1965 version of *The Greatest Story Ever Told* was the most costly movie ever filmed in America and its studio's biggest failure of that period (Hall 2002, p. 170)).

The difficulty of telling a Hollywood story about a protagonist with no character arc (he never changes his mind or alters any goals) seemed to leave Hollywood and the gospels at an impasse. Though the Jesus-freak, West End/Broadway theatrical successes inspired musical passions in the early 1970s (*Jesus Christ Superstar* (1973) and *Godspell: A Musical Based on the Gospel According to St. Matthew* (1973)), the Hollywood-studio Bible-epic cycle had come to an end. Most experiments with Jesus as the central protagonist have since been limited to television, where they receive less critical scrutiny and draw less controversy.

Filmmakers hoping for blockbusters turned instead to Christ-figure films and hit pay-dirt by adapting Joseph Campbell's monomyth as stories of Luke Skywalker and Superman. Such releases tend to make lots of money from the massive youth market; and they sound the conflicting calls of divine sacrifice and mundane urge, contemplating the mysteries of saviours incarnate. The plotting allows a hero with supernatural gifts and a unique calling to struggle with temptations and make repeated show of choosing duty over indulgence. This moves such heroes along character arcs with major decisions around which writers can structure involving stories. Fantasy franchises have their saviour cakes and eat them too by staying far from the gospels that Christians hold dear and rehearsing the struggles with more obviously fantastic characters instead: Luke Skywalker (Mark Hamill) of the *Star Wars* cycle, Neo (Keanu Reeves) of *The Matrix* cycle, Clark Kent (Christopher Reeve, Brandon Routh) of the *Superman* cycle, Aragorn (Viggo Mortensen) of *The Lord of the Rings*, Harry Potter (Daniel Radcliffe), etc. Audiences appear to adore them.

Conversely, the most popular epics to portray Christ himself (*The Robe*, *Ben-Hur*) steered clear of his inner life by regarding him from the points of view of others. The character arcs belonged not to Jesus but to those converted by their witness to his suffering. Tempted by sin but called to Christ, they pursue goals of selfish fulfilment and then climax their stories by turning to God instead. Both strategies, featuring Christ figures wresting with temptation, and onlookers to the original passion pulled toward salvation, have paid off.

Consider, by way of a contrast, the unhappy fate of *The Last Temptation of Christ*. In that plot, Jesus (Willem Dafoe) and Judas (Harvey Keitel) maintain a running debate about the saviour's mission; and, at each act break, Jesus changes his mind. Judas urges armed struggle against Rome, but Jesus first fears to do much of anything. Act One ends when the saviour announces that he has decided to travel and preach love. Act Two ends in high style when Jesus appears before his followers with Sacred Heart and an axe, to announce his shift from preaching love to doing battle instead. Act Three ends when he declares to a baffled Judas that he must give up rebellion and die on the cross. Act Four depicts the passion; having changed course thrice already, Christ despairs on that cross as a storm peaks and brings the act to a close. In the transition to the fifth and final act, the devil (Leo Marks) tempts Christ from his cross with a promise of comfort. Over the course of the climax, Jesus dreams of Magdalene's (Barbara Hershey) love and his own old age, but foresees that he would have to forsake his duty to accept such a life. He rejects this last temptation and succumbs to his painful death. Though the climactic temptation ends and returns the story to gospel accounts, it does so only after 160 minutes of Christ's changes of heart.

Either the forbidding length of this talky film, or the taboo sight of Christ in Magdalene's arms might have been enough to bore audiences and inflame conservatives; but Christian protestors at the time also rejected the portrayal of their saviour as unable to make up his mind. The filmmaker's failure to prescreen the film for the approval of suspicious evangelicals (such as Donald Wildmon, co-founder of the Moral Majority) began a chain of events that ended in picket lines, death threats against the Jewish executives of Universal Studios and the few instances of regional censorship since the Supreme Court outlawed it in 1952 (Lyons, 1996). I suggest not that any single element determined response to *The Last Temptation of Christ*, but merely that the portrayal of incarnated Christ as malleable to the point of being confused helped to limit Christians' approval. Though the notion of a saviour tempted from his duty has basis in gospel, it remains a side of his character on which orthodox viewers do not dwell.

The massive success of the Christ-figure films, alongside rejection of *The Last Temptation of Christ*, makes a case for a Hollywood rule: Do not use Jesus as a pivotal figure. If one wishes to structure a story around the temptations that saviours face, then do so with such surrogates as King Arthur, Superman, a Skywalker or Neo instead. Depictions of Jesus himself on screen should focus, for their character-arc motivations, on the mortals who are moved by the sacrifice of a strong and steady Christ.

If this theory is valid, then Benedict and Gibson made a profitable choice as they drafted their script for *The Passion of the Christ*. They focused on engaging protagonists and not just a sequence of events. The story hinges its act divisions on the movements of onlookers (Judas, Pilate, Simon) before climaxing with the crucifixion and the stalwart Christ redeeming them and defeating his tormentors. The plotting allows for long looks at Mary and Jesus but depends for progression on the frustrated pursuit of others' goals. And it does this without suggesting that God is unsteady enough to change his mind.

Still, formatting a script to solve one set of problems does not mean that no others will arise. Public response suggests that such plotting worked better for some viewers than for others. This focus away from Christ, along with the unexplained hostility of the Judean priests, bothered many people and maintained the polarization of its audience into supporters and opponents.

Undermotivation

Though Gibson compromised by subtitling most dialogue, he never meant the script to explicate the goals of anyone but Pilate. He preferred a visual narrative instead, and relied upon viewers to know the story and to receive the film as sacrament rather than exposition. This departure from Hollywood storytelling had the effect of making the film even more of a projective test than most tend to be; that is to say, audience members had unusual latitude to impute motives on the basis of prior learning from their respective communities. One consequence seems to have been a polarization of viewers. Conservative Christians could fill in the blanks with the Jew-blaming and violence familiar from their traditions. Scholars could critique the implicit theology of substitutionary atonement as conservative culture. And other groups could wonder what was going on and reject the story as unclear. Some did some or all of these at the same time; but the polarization of the audience (which enhanced this film's fortunes, as I have already argued) seems to have resulted, in part, from the ways in which they contributed to the story as they watched.

Even the supportive *Christian Century* noted drily that '*The Passion* works best when Christ is not onscreen' (Petrakis, 2004, p. 40). Many reviewers, for various groups' presses, complained that they learned little from the script about Jesus' intentions. The flashbacks to the last supper and sermon on the mount establish a message of love; but this Jesus says nothing of why he must suffer. A Catholic priest wrote that he 'found the character of Jesus strangely remote, almost a cipher ... for me the most troublesome aspect of the movie was its diminution of Jesus' ministry of teaching and healing' (Martin, 2004, p. 108).

The trade journal *Daily Variety* complained that

> Pilate is riven by conflicting pressures, some of which come from his wife, who is sympathetic to the persecuted Jewish firebrand. One of the limitations of Gibson's narrow time frame is that it doesn't allow for an explanation of how this has come to be so, unlike, for example, Nicholas Ray's 1961 'King of Kings'. (McCarthy, 2004, p. 39)

Such responses suggest that the demonstration of clear motivation, as developed by multiple scenes of exposition with significant characters, remains an important requisite to those who comment on feature films.

On the scholars' side, such authors as Paula Fredriksen apparently wished for a plot structured around Christ or his persecutors. She wrote that the story 'has no plot, no character development. We are never told why Jesus has to die, or why Caiaphas so desperately wants him to die, or why Jerusalem's Jews so insist on this death' (2006, p. 94). Other scholars likewise denounced the film for lacking complexity. Noting that at least Pilate struggles, Mark Douglas still complains that 'Gibson turns human beings into caricatures .... The disciples are always in mourning, most of the Sanhedrin are always bent on crucifying him' (2006, p. 136). The film critic for the *Christian Science Monitor* complained that 'the Jewish mob is portrayed as yowling for death with no hint of reason or rationality' (Sterritt, 2004). And other scholars have also noted that viewers were left to fill in the blanks with their own prior learning (Miller, 2006, p. 44; Thistlethwaite, 2004, p. 137).

I suggest on these bases that reception of the film was informed not only by the campaign that governed its release but also by the experience of the story as undermotivated. A plot structured around the failures of three onlookers (Judas, Pilate, Simon) to do more than sympathize was apparently not to the taste of many viewers, who wanted more of a sense of the motivations of Jesus and those who called for his death. One may speculate all manner of screenplay constructions that would have been more satisfying to such viewers; but, on the basis of the evidence at hand, we can conclude that the film left many to their own devices when it came to figuring out what those antagonists were up to.

That put conservative Christians at an interpretive advantage, in that the popular theology of substitutionary atonement afforded a view from which Jesus' actions made sense; and the habit of regarding Judean priests as aggressively hostile helped many of them with those otherwise undermotivated characterizations as well. Indeed, to conservative Christians such interpretations can seem obvious, to the extent that some may wonder why others do not see it. On his DVD commentary, Catholic apologist Gerry Matatics scoffs at

how silly the objections are, that the suffering is never given a context. Well, [the film] says, before you even see the action – you have that quote from Isaiah 53: 'He was wounded for our transgressions; he was bruised for our iniquities.' This is why everything you're about to see is happening. It's to solve the problem of our sins.

This Bible verse and its theological contexts are familiar to those in conservative Christian subcultures but viewers who approached the film from a background less well versed in the theology could easily become frustrated and impute a lack of plot, a lack of character or a lack of motivation. Sociologically, 'clear plotting' is both a professional norm within Hollywood and an outcome of alignment between the tellers of undermotivated stories and their audiences. To those who share a filmmaker's worldview and align themselves as members of his group, the story may make perfect sense, even if it focuses too fully on the one implicit idea; but to those outside the group, the story may appear not to be a story at all. The industry norm is to make stories clear to diverse audiences and so both demonstrate narrative skill and boost sales. In this case, owing to its independent production and alignment with a distinct subculture, filmmakers did not meet that Hollywood goal.

Though sympathetic reviewers voiced enough complaints about characterization to warrant a conclusion about the undermotivated script, there is one way in which the film did focus on a protagonist's attempt to meet a clearly dramatized goal. And given the controversy that drove response to the film, defeat of a sympathetic character's attempt to halt the execution bears closer analysis. I next dwell, therefore, on the decision of a reluctant Pilate to sentence Jesus to death at the end of Act Two. Within the context of the plot, this sentencing represents a failure. Pilate would like to free Christ but does not. For many viewers, the responsibility for that decision was the most sensitive aspect of the film. Discussion of the scene allows me to address the portrayals of Pilate and his Judean foils, and the larger debate about Jews and anti-Semitism that launched this film into the public eye.

✕ Part 5

KEY SCENE ANALYSIS

Synopsis

Setting: Plaza of the Roman Fort, day, shortly after the flogging and humiliation of Christ by Pilate's soldiers.

A crowd of Judeans talk among themselves. Pilate enters the colonnade above, sees Jesus' wounds, frowns at Abenader, and gently brings his prisoner forth to display to the mob. From her chambers, Claudia looks on in grief. Caiphas demands that the beaten Christ be crucified, to the approval of the crowd. Pilate responds, 'Isn't this enough?' Unable to placate the crowd, he asks Jesus to speak on his own behalf. But the prisoner replies that Pilate has no power save that given him from above, and that the greater sin is that of he who has brought him there. Caiphas shouts that Pilate's loyalty to Caesar requires that he crucify Jesus. Members of the mob grow more aggressive; and soldiers begin to beat them. Seeing this, Pilate sends for water. At the sight of the water bowl, Jesus recalls washing his own hands before his last supper with his disciples. Pilate cleans his hands and declares himself innocent of Jesus' blood. Claudia walks away in disgust, and Caiphas smiles. Pilate directs Abenader to 'Do as they wish.' The scene lasts four minutes twenty seconds and brings the second act to a close.

The scholars' review of the scripted face-offs between Roman and Judean[17] authorities over the fate of Christ resulted in some of their direst warnings of anti-Semitism. Close study of the final such confrontation allows me to analyze the filmmakers' responses to those warnings; to consider their adaptation of the sources they chose, their depictions of the motives of antagonists and the changes they made during production.[18]

As they composed the screenplay, Gibson and Fitzgerald drew material for this scene from the gospels of Matthew and John (the other two skip by the event quickly). From Matthew comes Pilate's washing of his hands, his line 'I am innocent of this man's blood; see to it yourselves' and the (mob's) spoken reply, 'His blood be upon us and on our children!' From the gospel of John, scenarists drew Pilate's presentation of the beaten Christ ('Behold the man!'), his exchange with Jesus ('Do you not know that I have the power to release you, and power to crucify you?' '... he who delivered me to you has the greater sin') and Caiaphas's taunt ('If you release this man, you are not Caesar's friend!').

The screenplay leaves out the backstory from the gospel of John, in which it is Caiaphas who fears the Romans rather than the other way around. A scene in the eleventh chapter of John introduces Caiaphas, who argues to his fellow priests that 'it is expedient for you that one man should die for the people, and that the whole nation should not perish'. John goes on to stipulate, lest a reader misunderstand the priest's intent, that

> He did not say this of his own accord, but being high priest that year he prophesied that Jesus should die for the nation, and not for the nation only, but to gather into one the children of God who are scattered abroad. So from that day on they took counsel how to put him to death. (John 11: 50–3)

My point is that the gospel provides no more reason to think that the priest would gloat over the sentencing of the condemned than it does to think that he could bully Pilate.

Instead of leaning on John for the scene, Gibson and Fitzgerald resorted to such sources as *The Dolorous Passion of Our Lord Jesus Christ*. That account, of the meditations of early nineteenth-century German nun Anne Catherine Emmerich, offers few concessions to anyone sensitive to anti-Semitism. Indeed, it specifies what the screenplay does not – the selfishness of the priests, whom it claims 'were actually dying for revenge' (2004, p. 143). Where Pilate is 'weak and undecided' (p. 217), the 'Jews' thirst for the death of Christ and pay his torturers to increase the cruelty of his punishment (p. 220). Pilate responds to the scourging of Christ with 'horror and compassion, whilst the barbarous priests and the populace, far from being moved to pity, continued their insults and mockery' (p. 237). Expressions of disdain for Jews and these depictions of them as cruel abound in the meditations; and Emmerich's memoirs report that Jews killed Christian babies for their blood (Schmöger, 1976, pp. 547–8). It reveals at least something of the screenwriters' approach that they set aside the Johannine account in favour of this version, and then later denied its anti-Semitism.

Indeed, Gibson responded with scorn to a reporter's query about descriptions of Jews in the Emmerich source:

> 'Why are they calling her a Nazi?' Gibson asked. 'Because modern secular Judaism wants to blame the Holocaust on the Catholic Church. And it's a lie. And it's revisionism. And they've been working on that one for a while.' (quote in Boyer, 2003)

Gibson appears to distinguish between the ancient Judeans, who include Jesus and Mary, and his critics among liberals, scholars and Anti-Defamation League personnel today. He shows sympathy toward the Judeans who followed Christ and remained apart from the group later called 'Jews'. But he seems suspicious, at the least, that the latter manipulate others, even to the point of war, with their inflated claims to victimhood. He thereby reverses the lesson of histories of the Holocaust. (He also voiced a blunter version of this theory – that Jews are destroyers of history and bringers of death – in spirited debate with the Malibu Sheriff's Department two years later, which I recount in the conclusion to this book.)

Whatever the role of Gibson's own feelings in construction of the script, the film makes it easy to see the priest as revelling in his domination of the Romans rather than as a responsible leader who feels that he must sacrifice one of his people to protect the rest from slaughter. In the film, Caiphas fears no one and says nothing of his intent. The smile he gives after voicing the Matthean curse suggests not relief that he has saved people from attack but glee at having bested his opponent. The gap between gospel and finished film is striking.

Via a series of events reviewed in Part 1 of this book, Gibson's team became defensive about the historicity of their work and maintained a stream of public comment – denial of any anti-Semitism – for years afterward. On the 'Theologian Commentary' of the *Definitive Edition* video release (2007), pundit

Screen capture: As Pilate washes his hands and Judeans shout for an execution, Caiphas smiles.

Gerry Matatics complains that, 'This is such a sensitive aspect of the movie for so many people, you know, it almost kind of muzzles us ... we have to be sensitive. And yet you can't rewrite history.' They have merely dramatized the gospel, the writers and theologians argue, and are therefore innocent of the charge. Such defence of a film on its video release suggests the ways in which filmmakers can market their work during a debate and long after conflict has ebbed. A close look at this scene, as narrated by Icon personnel in various media, can shed light on the relationship between the film's plotting, its makers' intentions, and its place in the larger controversy that shaped its classification and success.

The Finished Version

Comment on the sentencing scene has ranged from accounts of negotiations on the set and exposition of theology to ripostes to the charge of anti-Semitism. The last tell a very different story to those provided by the more mundane comments and details of the film. I contrast these to suggest that these attempts to rebut charges of anti-Semitism dissemble.

In *The Passion of the Christ*, the sentencing concludes a conflict between Judeans and Romans developed in prior scenes. An initial hearing by priests in their temple shows Caiphas to be resolute and manipulative. He stages a mock trial at night and looks on as his guards beat Christ and silence dissent. Later, he mocks Pilate's incapacity to control the noisy crowd, and leads his people to laugh at the governor. Caiphas shows no doubt about his desire to see Jesus put to death, at least until God's storm humbles him after the fact, and takes obvious pleasure in manipulating Pilate. By contrast, the Roman appears, in dialogue with wife Claudia, as relatively frail. He voices his fear of bloody punishment by Caesar should he resort to violence to quell a revolt. Though sensitive to Christ's words and his wife's entreaties, the film's Pilate suspects that mollifying Caiphas is his only safe move.

Though the sentencing lapses into scuffling between Romans and the Judean mob, most of the footage consists of a series of looks between officials and other contestants: Caiphas, the mob behind him, Pilate's right-hand man Abenader and Claudia. Compositions favour low shots, as if from below the colonnade, with which cinematographer Caleb Deschanel wished to convey the paradox of Pilate's historical significance as governor and helplessness before the crowd (Bailey *et al.*, 2004). Jesus remains marginal to the action, more spectacle than agent. Most tight shots focus instead on Pilate, as he notices Christ's wounds, reacts to the mob and glances at the wife whom he will disappoint.

Motivations go largely unstated, with dialogue limited to taunts and retorts and excluding statements of intent or references to the past. Actor Hristo Shopov is reported to have asked to play the governor as 'smooth' and 'gentle', and Gibson is reported to have agreed (Shepherd *et al.*, 2004). Jesus speaks to Pilate briefly of the greater guilt of the priests but otherwise remains silent; but because he bows his head for most of the scene, viewers have little access to his inner thoughts. The scene is Pilate's.

The governor enters and raises his eyebrows at the sight of Christ's wounds (a close-up emphasizes his reaction) and turns to Abenader, who opens his mouth and eyes wide as if embarrassed (earlier, Abenader had broken up the scourging of Christ in obvious anger at how far the torturers had gone). Pilate then displays the victim to the hollering crowd, with a gentleness that contrasts with the brutality shown by every other man who has touched him. After a medium shot displays Claudia's grief and disgust, Pilate speaks in obvious anger. When Caiphas growls for crucifixion and the crowd roars the demand in turn, a close-up on Pilate shows him frowning as if with

Screen capture: Pilate frowns at the sight of Christ's wounds.

Screen capture: Pilate frowns at Abenader, who opens his mouth as if to defend himself.

Screen capture: Pilate shows Christ's wounds to the crowd with a light touch.

Screen capture: Claudia responds with an expression of grief.

concern. He demands, 'Isn't this enough?' and asks that Jesus say something in defence of his life. But Jesus offers only that Pilate has no power and that the greater guilt rests with he who has brought him there.

Pilate's empathetic response is as striking as his anger over the abuse, in that he had ordered the scourging, stipulating that it be severe almost to the point of death. I infer from that earlier scene that he had planned to display

Christ's ravaged body in the hope that the extent of the violence would satisfy the Judeans. But Pilate does not proceed in such an instrumental way. The pause to display his sympathy and anger, over injuries that could work in his political favour, provides striking contrast to the jeers of the manipulative priests. While the Judeans yell for more, Pilate responds with a light touch to Christ's arm.

Pundit Gerry Matatics, on a running 'Producers' commentary included in the *Definitive Edition* video release, acknowledges these contrasting portrayals of Caiphas and Pilate and their roots in the Emmerich source.[19] He notes that Pilate is a point of audience attachment, a central figure in the sympathetic-onlooker plot:

> He's being pulled in two directions; and therefore I think, in a sense, Pilate serves as a paradigm for us. We're expected to see ourselves in him. What is our attitude toward Christ? Are you going to set him free or are we going to condemn him?

Matatics argues that Pilate appeases the wrath of the Judeans against his own impulse to treat Jesus gently, formed in conversation with his wife: 'In those scenes with Claudia', Matatics argues, 'he has a great respect for his wife. He trusts her intuition. … He's not just looking out for his own skin.'

Commenting on Jesus' remark to Pilate that 'He who handed me over to you has the greater sin', Matatics clarifies the bad light in which this casts the priests. He notes that

> we're reminded of a complementary truth in scriptures that there are degrees of sin; there are degrees of punishment in hell, degrees of reward in heaven. And there's a hierarchy there of degrees of culpability. Some are guiltier than others.

Matatics holds that the gospels first, and then such scenes in turn, rightly blame Judeans. Indeed, to the extent that mundane judgments of culpability rest on signs of malice aforethought, then guilt falls largely on the shoulders of the priest. Pilate, in contrast, is a relatively sensitive point of audience identification. The writers, actors and editing team seem to have gone out of their way to sway audience response in these directions.[20]

But this is not what those most directly involved in marketing have said about the film. Principal spokespeople, employed by Icon, have emphasized not Pilate's sympathy toward Christ and anger at those who abuse him, but his craven self-interest instead. Gibson's running commentary (on the *Definitive Edition* video release) emphasizes Pilate's relative lack of control and his fear of the consequences for him should priests and mob rise up. On his account, bolstered by screenwriter Benedict Fitzgerald, Pilate is not sensitive to the suffering Christ but merely afraid for himself. In these comments, as elsewhere, Gibson defends his plotting as transcription of gospel – as one supported by eyewitness accounts. Elaborating on the issue of Pilate's fear of Caiphas, for instance, Gibson refers to scant, ancient accounts of Josephus and Philo: 'Caesar had raked him over the coals twice for excessive cruelty in that province ... . So to say that he was in control was a little distorted, I think.' The argument is that Pilate cannot afford to allow Judeans to foment rebellion for fear of reprisals from Caesar, who would blame him for any failure to keep control without recourse to violence. (What would have motivated Caesar to hobble his own governor remains unclear, just as direct evidence that he ever did has yet to surface).

Steve McEveety (on the *Definitive Edition* 'Producer Commentary') follows suit, with complaints of being misinterpreted. He feels misunderstood by those who contrast a sensitive Pilate to the bloodthirsty Jews. He offers to correct audience impressions with his account that Pilate is

discovering the truth [of Christ's divinity] yet denying it, and therefore committing the worst sin of all. A lot of the audience didn't get that. Pilate is really – he's the bad guy ... and comes off as a nice guy.

Translator and dialogue coach Fulco maintains this argument, in line with the director and producer. Though he had reported from the set that Shopov and

Gibson agreed to emphasize Pilate's 'gentle' side (Shepherd *et al.*, 2004), Fulco later contradicted that account when (on the *Definitive Edition* video release) he counselled viewers on their interpretations of close-ups: 'Often, here, where Pilate seems gentle or more concerned, it is of course fear, not concern.'

Other denials of Pilate's relatively empathetic responses followed the film's release. For instance, Icon had Fr John Bartunek write a 186-page exposition, published as *Inside the Passion* (2005). Mostly concerned with theology, the author addresses the charge of anti-Semitism directly: the gospels represent impeccable sources of information, he claims, and only the most paranoid of viewers will see Caiphas as particularly villainous. Bartunek quotes Matthew on the envy that drives Caiphas and the film's faithful allusion to that (2005, p. 59). He invokes Gibson's historical analysis of Pilate as a weak ruler, cowed by Caesar from quelling rebellion with his usual force, vulnerable to manipulation by the priests (pp. 68–70).

Finally, Bartunek (2005) argues that Caiphas is not less concerned with suffering and truth but is simply more resolute and honourable than Pilate. Therefore, Bartunek suggests, the filmmaker cannot be charged with anti-Semitism. In his one direct comment on the negative light cast on the priest, Bartunek suggests that 'this criticism reflects more about the critics than about the film', and that 'if Pilate appears more sympathetic, it is only because it is easier for people today to identify with his lack of moral conviction … Caiphas, on the other hand, has deep moral convictions' (p. 83, n60).

I resort to this only for want of a better-reasoned reading, but these attempts to deny that Pilate is portrayed as sympathetic are disingenuous. They cast aspersions on viewers who sense anti-Semitism in the filmmakers' choices, in order to distract attention from the decisions made in choice of source materials, composition of the script, framing and performance on the set, and editing afterward. On screen, Pilate's combination of weakness and concern align him with Judas and Simon as the sympathetic onlookers around whom the larger plot turns. By contrast, Caiphas compares more closely to Satan and the most brutal soldiers as committing undermotivated evil (indeed, the final defeats are those of Caiphas and Satan, who weep in fear and rage in the dénouement). These alignments result from scripting, performance and editing decisions and not merely from misinterpretation by ignorant or amoral viewers. For filmmakers to claim that the historical Pilate feared the Judean high priest is unconvincing as historical argument but it is at least coherent. But to deny that Pilate appears to be the more concerned with the welfare of Christ is to dissemble. It runs counter to testimony by some of the film's supporters as well as the main source of the screenplay (Emmerich); contradicts dozens of reviews that comment on the portrayals; and makes nonsense of the plotting, editing and framing noted above. The filmmakers' denials that Pilate shows concern for his wife and for Christ appear to be hastily contrived responses to the accusations that blindsided them in April 2003. That they maintained them for years afterward suggests a congealed party-line that has become part of the marketing of a film in perpetual release. In Gibson's pre-release interviews, Bartunek's book and the *Definitive* home-video editions released years later, filmmakers take advantage of widely seen media and consumer durable products to give themselves (nearly) the last word on a sensitive topic, apparently hoping to clear their names. And for all of that, the portrayal of Pilate is not even the most sensitive issue in this scene.

Screen capture: The malevolent priest humbled by God at the end of *The Passion of the Christ*.

Caiphas's Curse

One of the major points of contention during the debate over anti-Semitism was the Matthean curse called down by Caiphas. On behalf of his people, he accepts collective blame for the crucifixion to come, in a manner often taken to justify Christians' persecution of medieval and modern Jews. Early critics of the script linked that line of dialogue to the violence that has sometimes been provoked by passion plays, and called for its removal (Boys *et al.*, 2003). Gibson appears to have been particularly upset by this demand.

In Matthew 25: 25, the crowd of Judeans appears to accept responsibility, pretty much as a community, for the execution of Christ, while Pilate washes his hands: 'His blood be upon us, and on our children.' The curse has long been a point of contention between Jewish and Catholic groups, the former often arguing that it is merely the anti-Semitic smear of evangelists who wish Jews to convert. Orthodox Christians have often retorted that any line appearing in the gospel is beyond critique. Understanding gospels to be true, and understanding themselves to be true to them, the filmmakers viewed any denial of the script's historical validity as an attack not merely on their filmmaking but on these pillars of Christendom as well. In a reversal that seems cruel in its historical irony, Jewish complaints about this Jew-blaming line came to seem like a Jewish attack on Christians.

By responding in that defensive manner, Gibson's team echoed the replies of DeMille, in 1927, to Jewish protests over *The King of Kings*. 'DeMille was not conciliatory' when B'Nai B'rith questioned his depiction of priests (Maltby, 1990, p. 209). After winnowing the scene between Caiphas and Pilate, and still drawing complaints from a rabbi with whom he worked, DeMille became fed up and wrote to the Motion Picture Producers and Distributors of America (MPPDA) with a complaint, and a threat, of his own. He wrote that he had told the rabbi that,

> I felt they would greatly harm the Jewish race by bringing the matter to the point of an open fight. I further stated to him that I did not want to

be forced to put in the title, 'his blood be upon us and upon our children's children,' nor any of the other titles that appear in the Gospels that might in any way be harmful to the Jews. ... You can see from all of the above that someone in the Jewish race is trying to start trouble. This trouble should be stopped immediately for the good of all, as it could very easily lead to a situation that might be very destructive.[21] Those Jews who are raising these rather violent objections would crucify Christ a second time if they had an opportunity, as they are so ready to crucify what, for want of a better term, I shall call His second coming upon the screen. (Maltby, p. 210)

Though the MPPDA attempted to be more conciliatory and prevent negotiations degenerating into a battle and mushrooming into scandal, a prominent rabbi went public with his fears, and public protests blighted DeMille's release, during a time when anti-Semitism was a more compelling issue for the industry than it had become by 2003. The release disappointed producers (p. 208), and no one would focus a Hollywood film on Jesus for decades – until the remake in 1961.

Events of 2003 replayed many of those of 1927: initial complaints based upon an early version of the project; a defensive response from a filmmaker disinclined to entertain critique from a Jewish group; public statements by offended parties; and so forth. Gibson mentioned feeling pressured by family not to give in too easily. As *New Yorker* reporter Boyer relates the deliberations:

Gibson shot the scene, but with Caiaphas alone calling the curse down. Wright, Gibson's editor, strongly objected to including even that version. 'I just think you're asking for trouble if you leave it in,' he said. 'For people who are undecided about the film, that would be the thing that turned them against it.'

Gibson yielded, but he has had some regrets. 'I wanted it in,' he says. 'My brother said I was wimping out if I didn't include it. It happened; it was said. But, man, if I included that in there, they'd be coming after me at my house, they'd come kill me' (Boyer, 2003).

Gibson's reference to scholars and the Anti-Defamation League fancifully rehearses DeMille's logic, in which any accusation of anti-Semitism amounts to an attack on Christ and those who love him.

Meanwhile, one of Gibson's defenders returned to DeMille's logic, that Jewish complaints can force Christian filmmakers to dig in their heels, that Jews themselves bear the responsibility for expressions of hostility against them:

> What did the ADL and its allies hope to accomplish with such bitter denunciations? The public condemnation of Gibson's movie made it less likely that he would re-edit the film to avoid offending the Jewish community. Given Gibson's often-expressed lofty intentions for his cinematic labor of love, how could he be seen as compromising his own vision of biblical truth for the sake of mollifying organizations and individuals who had already cried wolf over his alleged bigotry? (Medved, 2004, p. 40)

In fact, Gibson is reported to have wavered on a subtitled translation of the curse; but he finally excised it from the film and included it instead as a 'deleted scene' on the *Definitive Edition* video.

In that longer, older version, Caiphas smiles after speaking the curse; and Pilate executes one last show of defiance of the Judeans, by writing 'King of the Jews' on a sign to be affixed to the cross. This would seem to argue against the interpretation urged by Gibson, McEveety, Fitzgerald and Bartunek – that Pilate wishes merely to mollify his foes. That cut thereby furnished an even starker contrast between the relatively well-meaning Romans and the Judeans who scream for Christ's death. The inclusion of it as a 'deleted' extra on the *Definitive Edition* may function the way Pilate's sign does – as an act of defiance by a man intimidated by Jewish authorities, who dares not do what he wishes but who prevaricates instead and then settles for jabs at his foes. Setting aside the question of what counts as anti-Semitic portrayal,[22] it seems unlikely that the line taken in Gibson's publicity for this film – that filmmakers intended to portray Pilate as the most offensive villain – is anything more than a story conjured to sidestep accusations of bigotry.

The larger point, then, is that filmmakers must have felt compelled to dissemble in order to sell their film to the evangelical and conservative Catholic groups whose patronage would determine its success. What they originally intended when composing the script or shooting the film, I cannot guess. The screenwriters may have been nonplussed by the scholars' accusations of anti-Semitism in March 2003 (so Fitzgerald and Fulco report, in Shepherd et al., 2004). And any such dismay may have combined with organizational self-interest to create this pattern of denial and defensive denunciation.

In any case, Caldwell documents some of the follow-up to this public conflict between Gibson and his critics, which led to an upsurge in a current of American anti-Semitism that traditionally runs deep. At the time of the official release, www.SupportMelGibson.com greeted browsers with this bold headline: 'Why Do Jewish Leaders Want to Censor Mel Gibson?' The answer appeared below: 'In the current controversy, Mel Gibson is David against the Goliath of the anti-Christian Hollywood establishment and politically powerful Jewish leaders' (quoted in Caldwell, 2004, p. 214).

Not since protests against Universal's release of *The Last Temptation of Christ* in 1988 had such hostility toward Jews surfaced in discussion of popular film (a major protest in Hollywood featured a placard that read 'Jews 2', as if to indicate, following DeMille's logic, a second assault by the killers of Christ (Lyons, 1996, p. 306)). Resulting as it did from the work of a group of conservative Catholics insulated from the historical and Bible scholarship that might have helped them foresee the scandal to come; and marketed, as it was, to conservative Christians just as estranged from anti-defamation worldviews, the defensive promotion of the film wound up inciting more open expression of rancour toward Jews than any Hollywood film in years.

This contentious sentencing scene, distilling as it does a larger conflict over portrayals of respective authorities, and imputations of blame for the killing of Christ, serves not only as the pivotal moment of the film (it brings Act Two and Pilate's story to their ends) but also as the focus of the most significant scandal over a popular film in contemporary Hollywood history.

✖ Part 6

LEGACY

I have reviewed the principal debates and official decisions that attended release of this film. I have argued that it served as a touchstone in conflicts between professions and communities of faith. Depending on one's social ties, the various criticisms of the film were more or less likely to be viewed as admonitions to teach history with greater care (scholars), the smearing of artists' work (filmmakers), a defence of imperilled Jews (anti-defamation personnel and their liberal Catholic colleagues) or attacks on the kingdom of God (evangelicals and conservative Catholics). A rally of support frightened Jews whom evangelists have long sought to transform, and enriched an independent filmmaker beyond anyone's wildest dreams. Evangelical and conservative Catholics, in nations where churches are strong, appear to have impressed ratings boards with their resolve to take kids to the film. And evangelicals capitalized on the occasion to air their views about violence on screen – the fiery tool of conversion to faith that Hollywood wields for profit. All of this occurred in the context of heightened hostility, in the post-9/11 era, by evangelicals toward peoples of other faiths.

The style of the film's storytelling served a number of purposes: to avoid forcing Christ along a Hollywood character arc; to focus on bystanders who sense his importance but cannot avoid failing to help; and to appeal to Christians familiar with the gospels and able to fill in the blanks. Scenarists relied on anti-Semitic sources as they crafted the story on the page, on the set and in the editing bay. They leaned on Jew-blaming to an extent so remarkable that they were obliged to dissemble when people outside their groups called it to the world's attention.

I turn at last to the small legacy of the film, by recounting Icon's attempt at annual rerelease and the scandal that followed in its wake. My larger impression is that the world has returned to normal. The release was a notable blockbuster for groups who were, and continue to be, doing their jobs. Icon followed in the footsteps of decades of Jesus-film producers, merely adding a hostile response to Jewish criticism from which major studios would have shied, and focused on scenes of torture in an unprecedented way. We have no reason to think that mainstream filmmakers will follow in either direction.

In many ways, the bonds between the parties that had joined together for this blockbuster release frayed. Relations between Icon and the conservative Christian owner of Anschutz Entertainment Group – which controlled the huge cinema chain Regal Entertainment and mass-booked churches during the initial run – soured quickly. Months into release, Icon realized that churches had been charged $500 each for their group bookings. The fee for a private screening was standard Regal policy but was, perhaps unfortunately, labelled a 'worship fee', and lent the impression that Regal had snatched money from offering plates. Adding to this insult, Icon alleged injury in the form of tens of millions of dollars in profits that Regal had agreed to share but kept to itself. Icon sued and settled out of court just prior to the film's rerelease in 2005 (Szalai, 2005).[23] Indeed, many producers hoped to parlay support for Icon's film into further success with Christian viewers; but relations deteriorated in those ventures as well.

Icon was at the front of the line to expand Christian patronage of cinemas. Like George Stevens before it, who tried to turn *The Greatest Story Ever Told* into an annual rite worldwide (Hall, 2002), Icon planned annual releases to cinemas, and multiple home-video editions for showings elsewhere. The plan was to stimulate excitement and patronage among the faithful and the curious for years to come. And the initial DVD release was a huge hit, if short of the scale of family animated features (Hettrick and Ault, 2004).

Heeding the many calls from supportive Christians to reduce the intensity of the violence, Icon refashioned the film for wider consumption in 2005. The editors focused most of their attention on the set-piece scenes of torture, removing nearly all shots in which weapons strike flesh or blood drips from wounds, and most of those in which Christ cries out. They appear to have hoped that such reductions would yield a less restrictive rating in the US.

Screen capture: In footage trimmed from *The Passion Recut*, Jesus loses flesh to a soldier's flagellum.

But they were disappointed, in all likelihood because *The Passion Recut* looks less like a PG-13 than a run-of-the-mill R-rated movie. Having inspired CARA to suspend business as usual by marshalling Christian support with the marketing of its first release, Icon saw the administration return to normal the following year. Extended scenes of torture secure R ratings, pretty much no matter how they are cut. CARA told Icon that it would give the rerelease an R.

In what appears to have combined church-based marketing with pique, Icon released the new version unrated, at Easter 2005. That decision limited venues in which they could sell and screen the film, which may have been a major factor in its lack of success. Icon's marketing firms courted networks of churches rather than purchasing mass-media ads, but to little avail. No single reason arose for this decline in interest, though relations with the mass-booking chain Regal had soured. Church-group enthusiasm appears mainly to have petered out. Such bodies tend not to rally on behalf of filmmakers; depictions of torture do not usually sell to anyone but teens and horror buffs; and audience behaviour had returned to normal. Plans for annual showings in cinemas have been scrapped.

Others held out similar hopes that profits returned to Icon boded well for Christian-themed films. *Variety* reported an attempted revision of the industry two years afterward:

> To support the growing genre of faith-based movies, the industry has embraced an ever-growing set of guidelines described by some as the Passion Playbook. Among its edicts: Thou shalt woo the Bible Belt. Court the favor of local pastors. Avoid major media if they might send the wrong message. (Zeitchik, 2006, p. 14)

This push has enjoyed some successes but no massive reconfiguration of the industry. Tyler Perry has drawn the patronage of black Christians for his romantic comedies; Walden and Disney's adaptations of the C. S. Lewis fantasy *The Chronicles of Narnia* have enjoyed the blockbuster fortunes of the other Jesus-figure cycles that I reviewed in Part 4. But Christian films that do not fit these moulds have found only a niche market. Producer Steve McEveety left Icon to produce explicitly conservative Christian movies on his own, but so far without box-office success. At this point, it seems unlikely that independent producers will repeat Icon's triumph, at least with any regularity. Though the Anschutz Group owns both Walden (and its part of the *Narnia* adaptation) and many of the cinema screens in the US, and is unusually well capitalized in its bid to control media (Bunting, 2006), its dealings with Icon suggest that financial concerns will often trump evangelistic ones, in the upper reaches of blockbuster distribution as elsewhere in public life (Lindsay, 2006, p. 219). Hollywood continues to belong to the major, secular studios.

The other principals in this offscreen drama continue pretty much as they were, in their respective occupations: newspapers, talent agencies, universities, etc. They were doing their jobs then and continue to do so today. The biggest newsmaker remains the most notable still, though not always for the films that he makes. About two years after his film's initial run, Mel Gibson was detained by the law in Malibu – by a Jewish deputy, no less – for driving while intoxicated. Despairing that his life was 'fucked',

Gibson resisted arrest; and was subdued, manacled and recorded issuing a series of criticisms and threats to that deputy, including: 'Fucking Jews ... . The Jews are responsible for all the wars in the world ... . Are you a Jew?' (TMZ, 2006).

Press releases over the next few days offered apologies and assurances that Gibson did not really hate Jews. A couple of months later, he appeared on television to explain (Sawyer, 2006). He suggested that his thoughts, as he conversed with the deputy that night, had turned to war in the Middle East ('I remember thinking when I was twenty, "Man that place over there is going to drag us all into a black hole"') and to the debate over his film and feelings of persecution that it inspired:

> Even before anyone saw a frame of film, for an entire year, I was subject to a pretty brutal sort of public beating. And during the course of that, I think, I probably had my rights violated in many different ways (this is America), as an artist, as a Christian, just as a human being.

Apparently in reference to the violence that scholars and rabbis had predicted his movie would incite, Gibson noted that,

> The film came out and you could have heard a pin drop. Even the crickets weren't chirping. But the other thing I never heard was one word of apology. ... I thought I dealt with that stuff – all forgiveness. But the human heart's a funny thing. Sometimes you bear the scars of resentment, and it'll come out when you're overwrought.

Thus did the principal author reflect on his debate with scholars and Jews that had helped to clarify group boundaries and market his film. Whatever its ultimate source, Gibson's animosity, as he considered the film, remained focused on Jews. An undercurrent of American anti-Semitism, brought to the surface by scholars' complaints and the publicity campaign, had erupted again but has otherwise remained mostly hidden.

Life appears otherwise to have returned to professional norms for the filmmaker: buying and selling homes, running his company, clubbing with fans, cycling through mothers of his children, seeing private expressions turn into public gaffes and making new action movies. Like most everyone else involved with *The Passion of the Christ*, Gibson has maintained patterns of work typical of his profession, though subcultural revulsion at his streams of verbal bile has winnowed his choice of roles.

What of the evangelicals who embraced Gibson with such warmth and patronage? At first, it seemed like the support for his film might be strong enough to revive flagging churches:

> 'I don't know of anything since the Billy Graham crusades that has had the potential of touching so many lives,' said Morris H. Chapman, president of the executive committee of the Southern Baptist Convention, the nation's largest Protestant denomination. 'It's like the Lord somehow laid in our lap something that could be a great catalyst for spiritual awakening in this nation.' (quoted in Goodstein, 2004, p. 18)

Evangelists have long used less famous passion movies such as the *Jesus* video for worldwide proselytizing, and reported success in their work (Eshleman, 2002; Foer, 2004).[24] The language of violence is universal, and it makes religious stories compelling, even if evangelists sometimes differ over how much violence is ideal. Professionals in the field did seem to agree about the potential for Gibson's film. For example, a Texan pastor commented:

> I have no doubt that the movie will be one of the greatest evangelistic tools in modern day history. I think people will go to it and then flood into the churches seeking to know the deeper implications of this movie.[25]

However, Gibson's drunken lapse did little to help; and some of his supporters were taken aback. During the first week of coverage of Gibson's arrest, a critic of liberal Hollywood allowed that, 'Those of us who have defended and praised Gibson for his outspoken Catholic commitment, and for his efforts to use the movie medium to convey religious messages, feel inevitably betrayed and, yes, a bit humiliated' (Medved, 2006, p. 9).

This is not to suggest that evangelicals made any overt peace with critics and scholars, however. In a press statement of his own, evangelical lobbyist James Dobson stuck to his guns: 'Our endorsement of it stands as originally stated. We did not believe it was anti-Semitic in 2004, and our views have not changed.' Indeed, Dobson's public persona was founded in remaining steadfast in the face of any developments – a core meaning of *conservative*. And such stances may long define a subculture rooted in the rural South and hostile to secularism. Evangelical groups are vibrant parts of US life and are likely to remain so for decades at least.

Nevertheless, there are reasons to believe that the leadership of stalwarts like Dobson (who has since retired) has entered its twilight. Both scholars and group members observe trends that diminish the authority of such conservative icons: demographic shifts from the rural life that nurtured white, Gentile solidarity and its Christian fundamentalism; liberal backlash against the xenophobia of the Bush years; the assimilation that results from cultural engagement (Bishop and Cushing, 2008; Bruce, 1996; Noll, 2002; Shibley, 1996; Smith, 2003; Spencer, 2009). With the Republican Party out of executive power in the US (as of this writing, at least), one can at least conclude that the release of *The Passion of the Christ* effected no medium-term dominance of the values of the movement that sponsored it. Evidence of an awakening or political shift in their favour has yet to arise.

Indeed, the film inspired many to reflect on the marginal status of Jews and the Christian suspicions that maintain that, in political leadership in the US and elsewhere. This reflection led to the initial complaints that the film could provoke anti-Semitism. And during this decade, the religious boundaries of national identity have grown all the stronger among regular churchgoers, with consequences for political candidates whose Christianity they question (Straughn and Feld, 2010). But the tactical use of anti-Semitism, made by marketers of the film with what must be varying degrees of sincerity, has not resulted in sustained discussion. As a matter of public debate, the issue has largely faded from view.

A few months after the film opened, *Christian Century* writer John Buchanan reflected on the solidarity that the marketing campaign had inspired, which for a short time made the world seem as if divided in two: lovers of Christ impressed by the film, and liberal, Jewish and humanist critics. Buchanan wrote of the dilemma that evangelical activists face:

> I'd say there are two risks. The first is to turn our backs on the world, retreating to our sanctuaries and studies. This is, of course, an old and persistent temptation. The other risk is that we will pay too much attention to popular culture and, with the aim of being relevant and timely, simply mirror the culture's idolatries and preoccupations. (Buchanan, 2004, p. 3)

The motive to profit from an engagement with mass culture is strong ('our articles on that film generated more mail than did any other topic in years', he notes), as is the impulse to join the fray when conflicts erupt. But evangelicals may lose much of what defines them if they follow the money, pursue mass attention and work on Hollywood's terms.

Labouring in our own, competing institutions, scholars must forge a path through the same extremes, of insular scorn and dissolution of standards. Theologian Clive Marsh (2007) cautions against dismissing as trash any popular 'attempt to interpret the figure of Jesus' (p. 179) and suggests that we rise to such occasions by honing our 'media skills' (p. 180). Nevertheless, he also warns against selling out, reminding colleagues that they 'have a job to do … to limit what others would like to say about Jesus the Christ' (p. 181). We can revel in the attention and highs of blockbuster events, but must root claims in the solid ground of research lest we drift from scholarship into mundane reviewing and political comment. Hence, I have written this book, both to profit from controversy and to discipline talk of its context.

Scholars of film do well to embrace and affirm the import of bursts of public passion, and insist on disciplined history as a means to understand them. The soberest approach to this episode is to trace its roots through a century of Hollywood films about Christ and group struggles over them, to see how much of what happened amounts to business as usual. Against this backdrop, we can then also see how Icon's independence coupled with Gibson's stardom and hostilities, and their appeal to a reactionary group, to create an unusual hit out of what might have been a minor release. The filmmakers followed most Hollywood rules but with two exceptions (the antagonism and the bloodshed), and owe their success to a synergy of forces that operate at all times but never before in that combination. The storms of media focus, anti-Semitism, evangelical fervour and ritual violence having passed; survivors seem to have returned to business as usual.

We see these events in the light of film history, the workings of the global industry and the movements of audiences. Useful accounts of this film cannot result from even the most intensive interpretation by those withdrawn from public engagement or aloof to media fads. Nor can we assume that rushes of interest signal permanent shifts. Study of the routines of professionals and other groups will best measure the import and legacies of controversial films.

✖ APPENDICES

Appendix A: Key Details

Cast

Jesus	James Caviezel	Temple Guard	Adel Bakri
Mary	Maia Morgenstern	Thomas	Adel Ben Ayed
John	Christo Jivkov	James	Chokrl Ben Zagden
Peter	Francesco De Vito	Malchus	Roberto Bestazzonl
Magdalen	Monica Bellucci	Herod	Luca De Dominicis
Caiphas	Mattia Sbragia	Barabbas	Pietro Sarubbi
Annas	Toni Bertorelli	Dismas	Sergio Rubini
Judas	Luca Lionello	Gesmas	Francesco Cabras
Pontius Pilate	Hristo Naumov Shopov	Young Jesus	Andrea Ivan Refuto
Claudia Procles	Claudia Gerini	Cassius	Giovanni Capalbo
Abenader	Fabio Sartor	Janus	Matt Patresi
Joseph of Arimathea	Giacinto Ferro	Seraphia	Sabrina Impacciatore
Nicodemus	Olek Mincer	Young Girl	Daniela Poti
Woman in Audience	Sheila Mokhtari	Simon of Cyrene	Jarreth Merz
Old Temple Guard	Lucio Allocca	Baby	Davide Marotta
Whipping Guard	Paco Reconti	Satan	Rosalinda Celentano

Production Crew

Director	Mel Gibson	Additional Editing	William Hoy
Screenplay	Benedict Fitzgerald and Mel Gibson	Post-production Supervisor	Rajeev Malhotra
Producers	Mel Gibson, Bruce Davey and Stephen McEveety	Makeup Effects Consultant	Greg Cannom

Executive Producer	Enzo Sisti	Visual Effects	Ted Rae
Cinematographer	Caleb Deschanel	Supervisor/Second	
Production Designer	Francesco Frigeri	Unit Director	
Editor	John Wright	Theological Consultant	William J. Fulco, SJ,
Editor, *Recut*	Steve Mirkovich	and Aramaic/Latin	PhD
Music	John Debney	Translator	
Costume Designer	Maurizio Millenotti	Art Directors	Daniela Pareschi,
Special Makeup and	Keith Vanderlaan		Nazzareno Piana
Visual Effects			and Pierfranco Luscrì
Casting	Shaila Rubin	Sound Editors	Kami Asgar, Sean
Stunt Coordinator	Stefano Mioni		McCormack
Set Decorator	Carlo Gervasi	Sound Designer	Matt Temple
Music Supervisor	Peter Afterman		

Other Details

Production Company
Icon Productions

Shooting
Intensive pre-production, March 2002–November 2002. This includes location scouting, construction, casting and hiring of other personnel and contractors such as special-effects providers.

Exterior shooting, 4 November 2002–December 2002, Matera and Craco, Italy. This is the principal photography of exteriors of Christ's youth, the Via Dolorosa and wide shots of the crucifixion that required the setting of an ancient city.

Interior shooting and pickups, December 2002–March 2003, at Cinecittà Studios, Rome. This includes action in the Garden of Gethsemane, Judean temple, Roman fort and crypt as well as sacramental flashbacks and tighter shots of the crucifixion.

Post-production and reshoots, March 2003–January 2004, Los Angeles. This includes all editing, effects work, scoring and reshoots such as the sermon on the mount, photographed by the crew in Los Angeles in November 2003.

Appendix B: Releases and Ratings

Release Details

Initial cinema release, 25 February–July 2004, opening on 3,043 screens:

 US opening-weekend ticket receipts, $83,848,082
 US total ticket receipts, $370,274,604
 UK opening-weekend ticket receipts, £229,426
 UK total ticket receipts, £10,604,723
 Total ticket receipts outside the US, $241,116,490

Initial video release, 31 August 2004.
Cinema release of *The Passion Recut*, 11–31 March 2005, opening on 957 screens:

 US opening-weekend ticket receipts, $223,789
 US total ticket receipts, $508,326
 Total ticket receipts outside the US, $59,366

Definitive Edition DVD including *The Passion Recut*, 30 January 2007
Blu-ray version of *Definitive Edition*, 17 February 2009

Awards

The Passion of the Christ was nominated for Academy Awards in cinematography, makeup and music. In the US, it won '*Film of the Year*' awards from People's Choice, the Christian WYSIWYG Film Festival and the evangelical website *MovieGuide*.

Ratings, by Nation

Nation	The Passion of the Christ (2004)	The Passion Recut (2005)
Argentina	16	
Australia	MA-15	M
Bahrain	Banned (for visual depiction of a prophet)	
Brazil	14	
Canada	16+ (Quebec)	13+ (Quebec)
Canada	18A	
Chile	14	
China	Banned	
Denmark	15	
Finland	K-18	
France	12	
Germany	16	
Hong Kong	III – for persons aged 18 and above only	
Iceland	16	
India	A – public exhibition restricted to adults over 18	
Ireland	15PG	15A (15-video)
Israel	[Never picked up for distribution, never submitted for classification]	
Italy	T – all ages admitted	
Japan	PG-12	
Kuwait	Banned (for visual depiction of a prophet)	
Malaysia	Banned (except for Christians – tickets sold in churches)	
Mexico	C – for adults over 18	
Netherlands	16	
New Zealand	R16, reduced on appeal to R15	R15
Norway	15	
Peru	14	
Philippines	PG-13	
Poland	15	
Portugal	M/16	
Singapore	M18	
South Korea	15	
Spain	18	
Sweden	15	
UK	18	15
US	R (certificate #40366)	Unrated

Appendix C: Christian Watchdog Sites

Organizations that sponsor Christian movie reviews online include some shoestring ministries but also several expansive operations with institutional support (*Christian Spotlight*, an arm of Eden Communications; the *Film Forum* published by the magazine *Christianity Today*; *Plugged In*, published by Focus on the Family; and *Preview*, supported by Gospel.com and by readers' subscription fees). Some reviewers have professional media backgrounds in addition to church involvement. Dr Ted Baehr, the voice of the fee-based *MovieGuide*, has consulted for media organizations for years, written books and produced television shows. Phil Boatwright has a background in film criticism for news organizations, and now maintains the fee-based *Movie Reporter*.

Evangelical networks connect several of these sites. Michael Elliott contributed to Crosswalk.com and *Christianity Today*, and provided the *Movie Parables* for ChristianCritic.com until early 2008. Phil Boatwright of *Movie Reporter* also worked for the Dove foundation. Though the most independent small organizations (CAP and Cinema Focus) appear to be isolated, many of these sites are well situated among evangelical institutions. Jeffrey Overstreet is a Presbyterian layman who lent his reviewing to *Christianity Today* until it began to produce its own reviews in 2004. He now maintains *Looking Closer*. *MovieGuide* and *Plugged In* are the most conservative (and the most likely to be quoted in the mainstream media as voices of evangelicals or fundamentalists). *Movie Parables*, Looking Closer and *Film Forum* are the most cosmopolitan.

I compiled this table of thirteen sites by following links within evangelical networks and conducting internet searches.

Database	Host or affiliation	Year established
Childcare Action Project http://www.capalert.com/capreports/	Independent	2000
Christian Answers Spotlight http://www.christiananswers.net/spotlight/	Eden Communications	1995

Database	Host or affiliation	Year established
Christianity Today http://www.christianitytoday.com/movies/reviews	Christianity Today	2004
Cinema in Focus http://www.cinemainfocus.com/newreviews.htm	Methodist	2003
Crosswalk http://www.crosswalk.com/movies/archives/	A 'for-profit religious corporation'	2001
Dove Foundation http://www.dove.org/reviews/	Independent	1995
Looking Closer http://lookingcloser.org/film-review-archive/	Promontory Artists/ Presbyterian	2000
MovieGuide http://www.movieguide.org/	Independent	1994
Movie Parables http://www.christiancritic.com/	Christian Critic	1998–2008
Movie Reporter http://www.moviereporter.com/	C.C. Publications	1998
Planet Wisdom http://www.planetwisdom.com/movies/	WisdomWorks Ministries	1999
Plugged In http://www.pluggedinonline.com/movies/	Focus on the Family	1999
Preview http://www.previewonline.org/	Gospel.com/an 'inter- denominational church'	1993

Note: I italicize review databases that appear as publications supported by larger organizations (as in the case of *Plugged In*, a publication of Focus on the Family). Other review sites are independent and are not italicized.

Appendix D: Notes

1 One can be a scholar without worrying whether historians at Harvard or Stanford will approve of one's work. Many evangelicals work at Bible colleges and seminaries. But, whatever the overlaps, they also move in very different networks of disciplined scholarship. For instance, a defence of Icon's film from liberal Jewish rebuke issued from Rikk Watts (2004), New Testament teacher at the British Columbian Regent College.

2 A spokesperson for the Society of St Pius X comments on Jewish culpability:

> We just hold to what the church has always held ... . The physical crucifixion was performed by the Romans, but it was the Jews who urged the Romans to do it, as the Bible says. The Jews were the ones who sought the crucifixion, so in a certain sense they're responsible for it. They were the ones who condemned him, but they didn't have the power to crucify him, so they got the Romans to do it.

What attitude toward Jews results?

> We want people to become Catholic. The Lord himself was a Jew. We have no animosity toward Jews. We want them to see the full truth. The Lord came to show them, but not everyone was willing to see it. (Brown, 2004).

Traditionalists appear to love Jews enough to want them to cease to be Jews.

3 In his history of the promotion and failure of *The Greatest Story Ever Told*, Hall suggests that the roadshow epic business model was unworkable in that it allotted huge budgets for prestige films but provided no brake on filmmakers' largess (2002, p. 183). Indeed, that model fell apart after nearly bankrupting major studios at the end of the decade. Though the blockbuster years (mid-1970s and beyond) would revive the massive budget, it would do so only on behalf of youth-oriented action spectacles that have proved to sell well worldwide. I return in Part 4 to the difference between the Jesus movie proper and the Christ-figure fantasy that sells around the world.

4 For examples from the previous decades, see before-and-after version of attacks in such Hollywood films as *Menace II Society* (1993), *Natural Born Killers* (1995), *Scream* (1996) and *True Romance* (1993). In order to win R ratings, editors trimmed any shots or brief sequences in which enthusiastic assailants fire more than one shot or stab someone more than once in acts of one-on-one violence.

5 The multi-religious nation of Singapore employed a new rating system with the release of *The Passion of the Christ*, branding it M18 rather than restricting it to those over twenty-one years of age.

6 Of evangelism in the US, the *New York Times* reported that,

> Ron Luce, president of Teen Mania [an evangelical group that stages crusades in stadiums], says children would benefit from seeing it, and the CD ROM [kits that instruct young people in how to use the film to deepen their faith and bring friends to Christ] supplies information to persuade parents to allow their children to attend. (quoted in Goodstein, 2004, p. 18)

7 As conflict developed, some groups drew boundaries with increasing clarity. In the year following this controversy, the Society has made it clear that they regard Hastings as driven in his deliberation as Censor in part by his status as 'an openly "gay" man' (SPCS, 2005).

8 Christian media watchdogs have long drawn this distinction between low and high, in reference to torture or to entertainment in general. In his analysis of passion plays, Musser documents the drawing of 'highly superficial but widely observed distinctions':

> Travel lectures were usually presented to genteel audiences in churches, whose members disapproved of idle amusement in any form. Such lectures were customarily understood to transport spectators to a distant place for the purpose of inspiring or educating them. The local theater, on the other hand, was seen as importing the exotic, the foreign, and the sensational to titillate its patrons and stimulate their desires and fantasies. (1996, p. 57)

Thus, in Musser's account, filmmakers gained licence to present Christ on film in ways that could move viewers without drawing wide condemnation as titillation.

9 For a general discussion of distinctions in culture, see Bourdieu (1984); and, for an application to evangelicals, see Lindsay (2006), who found that graduation from elite academies and mentions of high-end literature serve as markers of cultural capital for evangelical social climbers from Harvard to Hollywood.

10 I refer to the Tennessee prosecution of a teacher of evolution, by which public trial many fundamentalists were humiliated as superstitious and ignorant (McGowen and Feinberg, 1990; Regnerus and Smith, 1998).

11 For scholarly discussions, albeit from opposing disciplinary and ideological poles, see Bushman and Anderson (2001); Murdock (1997); Potter (2003); Springhall (1998); Starker (1989).

12 Reviewers probably did not know, at that time, that Gibson had returned to his family's conservative Catholicism.

13 Rubenstein cites a phantom article attributed to the *Jerusalem Post*, which citation appears, in my own research, to derive from an email hoax. The story – of a young Gibson's conversion to Orthodox Judaism and subsequent deprogramming by his anti-Semitic father

– appears to be too juicy to be true. I suggest that the fever-pitch solidarity inspired by struggles with Icon and evangelicals may have raised the willingness of even the most eminent and accomplished scholars to accept reports of psychological instability on the opponent's side.

14 Analysts (Bordwell *et al.*, 1985) have demonstrated that large numbers of Hollywood feature films adhere to classical principles of character-driven drama. Thompson (1999) shows that contemporary films break their stories into sets of acts (usually four per 90–150-minute feature, rather than the three claimed by Syd Field in his famous 1979 text), which emphasize character traits at their conclusions.

15 This may help to answer the oft-put question as to why evangelicals embrace so Marian a film (e.g., Neff, 2004, p. 34). Mary is front and centre but has no effect on anyone and nothing to do with the film's goal-driven plot, and therefore cannot be said to act out any doctrines to which Protestants object. Jesus takes the occasional moment of courage by looking into his mother's eyes, but does not change his course of action in response. The four women with speaking roles (Mary, Magdalen, Claudia and the Veronica-figure Seraphia (Sabrina Impacciatore)) most closely fit the image of colonial femininity described by Richard Dyer in his study of whiteness on film (1997): There is nothing they can do but weep and suffer before the injustice they see. Their white, feminine beauty is anchored in their impotence. Where the male protagonists of the plot betray, condemn, and assist with the cross – each literally or figuratively pushing the action forward – powerless women stand by and then help clean up the mess.

16 In what appears to result from difficulty with digital composites, the post-production teams have given Christ what I can only think to call *mood eyes*, which shift in hue from shot to shot. They change from Caviezel's own blue (as in this frame), to a yellowish brown, to a reddish purple. I have found no commentary on this unusual characterization and regard it as a distracting result of having cast yet another blue-eyed Gentile as the Semitic Christ.

17 Scholars extend their historical treatment of Biblical text to such pronouns as 'Jews', which many regard as a term of opposition. They argue that early Christians coined the term decades after the time of Christ, to refer to people from Judea who either condemned Jesus during his life (e.g., the temple elite in Jerusalem) or who refused to follow him decades later when the gospels were written (Meacham, 2004, p. 6; Reinhartz, 2002, pp. 112–14).

18 Icon has been unwilling to distribute copies of screenplay drafts, restricting the present analysis to the account of an early script provided by the *ad hoc* committee of scholars (Boys *et al.*, 2003), Boyer's reporting (2003), the finished film and statements made about it *post hoc*.

19 These respective portrayals also match those of the Lenten play in which my mother performed (Mueller, 1993). The priest is described in animal terms ('rat', 'lice') and exhibits no ambivalence over having bribed crowds to shout for a killing. Pilate, chastised by his angry wife, shows much regret. Dramatically, the priest is a foil for the spiritual growth of others – an example of untempered malice – whereas audiences might see themselves in weak-willed Pilate, cowed from doing what he knows to be right.

20 In an example of that interpretation of Pilate as kinder than Caiphas, an evangelical minister argues that Gibson might be forgiven the portrayal of the priests as

> dealing with the action of a few, which cannot be globalized into collective guilt of some kind. But the portrait of Pilate is another matter ... his Pilate seems weak, indecisive, even tormented ... the biblical motif of Pilate's washing his hands ... signaling Pilate's fair-mindedness. (Witherington III, 2004, pp. 86–7)

21 This threat found voice among evangelicals during the fall 2003 marketing campaign: 'the campaign to brand The Passion as anti-Semitic with a potential "tinderbox effect" is dangerous to Jews ... evangelicals are tempted to react with anger to allegations of bigotry' (*Christianity Today*, 2003, p. 43).

22 Segal (2004, pp. 197–9) provides extended discussion, offering provisional definitions of *anti-Judaism* (ancient evangelical arguments against theological competitors) and *anti-Semitism* (either a modern, Nazi genocidal aggression against a race, or an older view of Jews as supernaturally evil and collectively accountable for the death of Christ). He concludes that *The Passion of the Christ* is surprisingly and gratuitously anti-Semitic in the latter sense. He also expresses his hope that Gibson would *not* include the blood curse as a deleted scene in video release (p. 203) – a hope that turns out to have been in vain.

23 Lawsuits over fees are business as usual in Hollywood. Icon settled one with writer Fitzgerald, over his compensation, in the spring of 2009.

24 Production of the *Jesus* film occurred in 1978–9, funded by the evangelical organization Campus Crusade for Christ (CCC) and executed by Hollywood producer John Heyman, who had been making short films of Bible stories for years. Warner Bros. handled the unprofitable commercial distribution; and CCC has since translated and shown the film in missionary work around the world.

25 *Ed Young Jr, Pastor, Dallas-Area Fellowship Church*, quoted online at http://www.thepassionoutreach.com/quotes.asp.

Appendix E: References

Abramowitz, R. (2004) 'Gibson Talks about Film, Furor and Faith', *Los Angeles Times*, 15 February, p. A1.

Achterberg, P., Houtman, D., Aupers, S., Koster, W. de, Mascini, P. and Waal, J. van der (2009) 'A Christian Cancellation of the Secularist Truce? Waning Christian Religiosity and Waxing Religious Deprivatization in the West', *Journal for the Scientific Study of Religion* vol. 48 no. 4, pp. 687–701.

AFP (2004) 'Gibson Film Stirs Religious Controversy in Kuwait', 29 March. Available from: http://www.middle-east-online.com/english/culture/?id=9432 (accessed November 2008).

Agreda, M. de and Blatter, G. J. (1971) *City of God: The Conception; the Divine History and Life of the Virgin Mother of God, Manifested to Mary of Agreda for the Encouragement of Men*, Ypsilanti, MI: Ave Maria Institute.

Ansen, D. (2004) 'So What's the Good News?', *Newsweek* vol. 143 no. 9, p. 60.

AsiaNews.it (2004a) 'Malaysian Muslims Offended by "The Passion"', 5 April. Available from http://www.asianews.it/index.php?l=en&art=584&dos=16&size=A (accessed December 2008).

Bailey, J., Pizzello, S. and Bosley, R. K. (2004) 'A Savior's Pain' (Interview), *American Cinematographer* vol. 85 no. 3, pp. 48–61.

Bartunek, J. (2005) *Inside the Passion: An Insider's Look at The Passion of the Christ*, West Chester, PA: Ascension Press.

Bensinger, K. (2004) 'Mexico Nails Over-18 Rating on "Passion"', *Daily Variety* vol. 282 no. 55, p. 8.

Bensinger, K., Birchenough, T., Groves, D., Klaussmann, L., Meza, E., Newbury, C. *et al.* (2004) '"Passion"-Bashing Minimal', *Variety* vol. 394 no. 10, pp. 8–14.

Bishop, B. and Cushing, R. G. (2008) *The Big Sort: Why the Clustering of Like-Minded America Is Tearing Us Apart*, Boston, MA: Houghton Mifflin.

Bordwell, D. (2006) *The Way Hollywood Tells It: Story and Style in Modern Movies*, Berkeley: University of California Press.

Bordwell, D., Thompson, K. and Staiger, J. (1985) *The Classical Hollywood Cinema: Film Style and Mode of Production to 1960*, New York: Columbia University Press.

Bourdieu, P. (1984) *Distinction: A Social Critique of the Judgement of Taste*, Cambridge, MA: Harvard University Press.

Boyer, P. J. (2003) 'The Jesus War', *New Yorker*, 15 September.

Boys, M. C. (2004) 'Seeing Different Movies, Talking Past Each Other', in J. Burnham (ed.) *Perspectives on The Passion of the Christ: Religious Thinkers and Writers Explore the Issues Raised by the Controversial Movie*, New York: Hyperion.

Boys, M. C., Cook, M. J., Cunningham, P. A., Fisher, E. J., Fredriksen, P., Frizzell, L. E. *et al*. (2003) *Report of the Ad Hoc Scholars Group: Reviewing the Script of* The Passion.

Brooks, C. and Manza, J. (2004) 'A Great Divide? Religion and Political Change in U.S. National Elections, 1972–2000', *Sociological Quarterly* vol. 45 no. 3, pp. 421–50.

Brottman, M. (1997) *Offensive Films: Toward an Anthropology of Cinéma Vomitif*, Westport, CT: Greenwood Press.

Brown, E. (2004) 'Beyond the Trappings', *Los Angeles Times*, 15 February. Available from: http://www.latimes.com/news/local/valley/la-tm-catholics07feb15,0,2607921.story (accessed November 2008).

Bruce, S. (1996) *Religion in the Modern World: From Cathedrals to Cults*, New York: Oxford University Press.

Buchanan, J. M. (2004) 'Up for Review', *Christian Century* vol. 121 no. 11, p. 3.

Bunting, G. F. (2006) 'A Denver Billionaire's Invisible Hand', *Los Angeles Times*, 23 July. Available from: http://articles.latimes.com/2006/jul/23/local/me-anschutz23 (accessed December 2008).

Burnham, J. (ed.) (2004) *Perspectives on The Passion of the Christ: Religious Thinkers and Writers Explore the Issues Raised by the Controversial Movie*, New York: Hyperion.

Bushman, B. J. and Anderson, C. A. (2001) 'Media Violence and the American Public: Scientific Facts versus Media Misinformation', *American Psychologist* vol. 56 no. 6, pp. 477 89.

Caldwell, D. (2004) 'Selling Passion', in J. Burnham (ed.) *Perspectives on The Passion of the Christ: Religious Thinkers and Writers Explore the Issues Raised by the Controversial Movie*, New York: Hyperion.

Caputi, J. (1989) 'The Sexual Politics of Murder', *Gender & Society* vol. 3 no. 4, pp. 437–56.

Chartrand, H. F. (2004) 'Jewish Actors: Gibson's "Passion" Not Anti-Semitic', *Jerusalem Post*, 14 January, p. 24.

Christianity Today (2003) 'Jews against Jesus?', *Christianity Today* vol. 47 no. 11, p. 43.

Cobb, J. (2004) Marketing 'The Passion of the Christ', *MSNBC*, 25 February. Available from: http://www.msnbc.msn.com/id/4374411/ (accessed 14 April 2009).

Cole, C. (1960) 'Problems for Producers over Full View Christ', *Films and Filming* vol. 6 no. 7, p. 27.

Daily Variety (2003) 'Let "Passion" Play', *Daily Variety* vol. 280 no. 18, p. 19.

Dart, J. (2003) 'Gibson's Passion Gets an Evangelical Blessing', *Christian Century* vol. 120 no. 15, p. 14.

Dart, J. (2004) 'Passion, Judas Present Contrast in Jesus Films', *Christian Century* vol. 121 no. 4, pp. 15–16.

Dobson, J. (2004) 'The Greatest Story Ever Told', *Dr. Dobson's Newsletter*, February. Available from http://www.family.org/docstudy/newsletters/a0030580.cfm (accessed May 2005).

Douglas, M. (2006) 'The Passions of the Reviewers', In T. K. Beal and T. Linafelt (eds) *Mel Gibson's Bible*, Chicago, IL: University of Chicago Press.

Dyer, R. (1997) *White*, New York: Routledge.

Ebert, R. (2004) *The Passion of the Christ*, 24 February. Available from: http://rogerebert.suntimes.com/apps/pbcs.dll/article?AID=/20040224/REVIEWS/4022403 01/1023 (accessed 12 March 2009).

Emmerich, A. C. (2004) *The Dolorous Passion of Our Lord Jesus Christ*, El Sobrante, CA: North Bay Books.

Enders, J. (2006) 'Seeing Is Not Believing', in T. K. Beal and T. Linafelt (eds) *Mel Gibson's Bible*, Chicago, IL: University of Chicago Press.

Eshleman, P. A. (2002) 'The "Jesus" Film: A Contribution to World Evangelism', *International Bulletin of Missionary Research* vol. 26 no. 2, p. 68.

Evans, J. (1996a) 'Calling Christians to Righteousness in Their Movie/TV Viewing', *Preview*. Available from: http://www.gospelcom.net/preview/subpgs/artcoms/callright.html (accessed March 2002).

Evans, J. (1996b) 'How Movie Morality Ministries Evaluate Movies and TV Shows', *Preview*. Available from: http://www.gospelcom.net/preview/subpgs/artcoms/callright.html (accessed March 2002).

Felson, R. B. (1996) 'Mass Media Effects on Violent Behavior', *Annual Review of Sociology* vol. 22 no. 1, pp. 103–28.

Fine, J. and Osborne, M. (2004) ' "Passion" Uncut for Egypt, Singapore Bows', *Daily Variety* vol. 282 no. 63, p. 6.

Fitzgerald, B., Fox, R., Fulco, W., Nicolosi, B. and Turan, K. (2004) *Whose Passion? Media, Faith & Controversy*, Conference, 3 March, University of Southern California.

FLBR (2004) *Decision of the Film and Literature Board of Review: Decision Number One*, Wellington, New Zealand: Film and Literature Board of Review.

Foer, F. (2004) 'Baptism by Celluloid', *New York Times*, 8 February, Arts1, p. 26.

Fredriksen, P. (2003) 'Mad Mel: The Gospel According to Gibson', *New Republic* vol. 229 nos 4/5, pp. 25–9.

Fredriksen, P. (2004) 'Responsibility for Gibson's *Passion of Christ*', *Responsive Community* vol. 14 no. 1, pp. 59–63.

Fredriksen, P. (2006) 'No Pain, No Gain?', in T. K. Beal and T. Linafelt (eds) *Mel Gibson's Bible*, Chicago, IL: University of Chicago Press.

Freedman, J. L. (2002) *Media Violence and Its Effect on Aggression: Assessing the Scientific Evidence*, Toronto, ON: University of Toronto Press.

Gates, D. (2004) 'Jesus Christ Movie Star', *Newsweek* vol. 143 no. 10, 7 March, p. 50.

Gomery, D. (1998) 'Hollywood Corporate Business Practice and Periodizing Contemporary Hollywood History', in S. Neale and M. Smith (eds) *Contemporary Hollywood Cinema*, New York: Routledge.

Gomery, D. (2003) 'The Hollywood Blockbuster: Industrial Analysis and Practice', in J. Stringer (ed.) *Movie Blockbusters*, New York: Routledge.

Goodstein, L. (2003) 'Months before Debut, Movie on Death of Jesus Causes Stir', *New York Times*, 2 August, A1, p. 10.

Goodstein, L. (2004) 'Some Christians See "Passion" as Evangelism Tool', *New York Times*, 5 February, A1, p. 18.

Greenberg, E. J. (2003a) 'The "Passion" of Mel Gibson: Hollywood Star and Fundamentalist Catholic's Telling of the Last Hours of Jesus' Life Has Jewish, Interfaith Leaders Anxious', *The New York Jewish Week*, 28 March, pp. 57–61.

Greenberg, E. J. (2003b) 'Jews Horrified by Gibson's Jesus Film', *New York Jewish Week*, 15 August, pp. 1–11.

Grieveson, L. (2004) *Policing Cinema: Movies and Censorship in Early-Twentieth-Century America*, Berkeley: University of California Press.

Guth, J. L., Kellstedt, L.A., Smidt, C. E. and Green, J. C. (2006) 'Religious Influences in the 2004 Presidential Election', *Presidential Studies Quarterly* vol. 36 no. 2, pp. 223–42.

Halevi, Y. K. (2004) 'Jews and Christians after "The Passion"', *Jerusalem Post*, 5 March, p. 21.

Hall, S. (2002) 'Selling Religion: How to Market a Biblical Epic', *Film History* vol. 14 no. 2, pp. 170–85.

Heschel, S. (2006) 'Christ's Passion: Homoeroticism and the Origins of Christianity', in T. K. Beal and T. Linafelt (eds) *Mel Gibson's Bible*, Chicago, IL: University of Chicago Press.

Hettrick, S. and Ault, S. (2004) 'Dvd Buyers Express "Passion" (Cover Story)', *Daily Variety* vol. 284 no. 42, p. 1.

Hout, M. and Fischer, C. S. (2002) 'Why More Americans Have No Religious Preference: Politics and Generations', *American Sociological Review* vol. 67 no. 2, pp. 165–90.

James, R. (2009) 'Narnia as a Site of National Struggle: Marketing, Christianity, and National Purpose in *The Chronicles of Narnia: The Lion, the Witch and the Wardrobe*', *Cinema Journal* vol. 48 no. 4, pp. 59–76.

Kennedy, R. (2004) '"Passion" Film Is Incendiary, 2 Jewish Leaders Report', *New York Times*, 23 January, A12.

Kermode, M. (2004) 'The Passion of the Christ', *Sight and Sound* vol. 14 no. 4, pp. 62–3.

LaBelle, B. (1980) '*Snuff* – the Ultimate in Woman-Hating', in L. Lederer (ed.) *Take Back the Night: Women on Pornography*, New York: Morrow.

Levine, A.-J. (2004) 'First Take the Log out of Your Own Eye: Different Viewpoints, Different Movies', in J. Burnham (ed.) *Perspectives on The Passion of the Christ: Religious Thinkers and Writers Explore the Issues Raised by the Controversial Movie*, New York: Hyperion.

Levinson, C. (2004) 'Arab Censors Giving "Passion" Wide Latitude', *San Francisco Chronicle*, 1 April. Available from: http://www.sfgate.com/cgi-bin/article.cgi?file=/c/a/2004/04/01/MNGH35UO881.DTL (accessed December 2008).

Lindlof, T. R. (1996) 'The Passionate Audience: Community Inscriptions of *The Last Temptation of Christ*', in D. A. Stout and J. M. Buddenbaum (eds), *Religion and Mass Media: Audiences and Adaptations*, Thousand Oaks, CA: Sage.

Lindsay, D. M. (2006) 'Elite Power: Social Networks within American Evangelicalism', *Sociology of Religion* vol. 67 no. 3, pp. 207–27.

Linnell, G. (2006) '"Applauding the Good and Condemning the Bad": *The Christian Herald* and Varieties of Protestant Response to Hollywood in the 1950s', *Journal of Religion and Popular Culture* vol. XII. Available from: http://www.usask.ca/relst/jrpc/art12-goodandbad.html (accessed December 2008).

Lyons, C. (1996) 'The Paradox of Protest: American Film, 1980–1992', in F. G. Couvares (ed.) *Movie Censorship and American Culture*, Washington, DC: Smithsonian Institution.

MacDonald, G. J. (2004) '"Passion" Rekindles Debate over Meaning of the Crucifixion', *Christian Science Monitor* vol. 96 no. 62, p. 1.

MacKinnon, C. A. (1989) *Toward a Feminist Theory of the State*, Cambridge, MA: Harvard University Press.

Malbon, E. S. (2000) *In the Company of Jesus: Characters in Mark's Gospel*, 1st edn, Louisville, KY: Westminster John Knox Press.

Maltby, R. (1990) 'The King of Kings and the Czar of All the Rushes: The Propriety of the Christ Story', *Screen* vol. 31 no. 2, pp. 188–213.

Márquez, J. (2006) 'Lights! Camera! Action!', in T. K. Beal and T. Linafelt (eds) *Mel Gibson's Bible*, Chicago, IL: University of Chicago Press.

Marsh, C. (2007) 'Why the Quest for Jesus Can Never Only Be Historical: Explorations in Cultural Christology', *Louvain Studies* vol. 32 nos 1–2, pp. 164–81.

Marshall, D. A. (2002) 'Behavior, Belonging, and Belief: A Theory of Ritual Practice', *Sociological Theory* vol. 20 no. 3, pp. 360–80.

Martin, J. (2004) 'The Last Station: A Catholic Reflection on *The Passion*', in J. Burnham (ed.) *Perspectives on The Passion of the Christ: Religious Thinkers and Writers Explore the Issues Raised by the Controversial Movie*, New York: Hyperion.

Marvin, C. and Ingle, D. W. (1999) *Blood Sacrifice and the Nation: Totem Rituals and the American Flag*, New York: Cambridge University Press.

McCarthy, T. (2004) 'An Unrelenting Cross to Bear', *Variety* vol. 394 no. 2, pp. 2, 39.

McGowen, T. and Feinberg, B. S. (1990) *The Great Monkey Trial: Science versus Fundamentalism in America*, New York: Franklin Watts.

McNary, D. (2005) 'Mel Rewards the Faithful', *Variety* vol. 398 no. 4, p. 3.

Meacham, J. (2004) 'Who Really Killed Jesus?', in J. Burnham (ed.) *Perspectives on The Passion of the Christ: Religious Thinkers and Writers Explore the Issues Raised by the Controversial Movie*, New York: Hyperion.

Medved, M. (2004) 'The Passion and Prejudice', *Christianity Today* vol. 48 no. 3, pp. 38–41.

Medved, M. (2006) 'Reconciliation Should Follow Mel's Malibu Meltdown', *USA Today*, 3 August, p. A9.

Merino, S. M. (2010) 'Religious Diversity in a "Christian Nation": The Effects of Theological Exclusivity and Interreligious Contact on the Acceptance of Religious Diversity', *Journal for the Scientific Study of Religion* vol. 49 no. 2, pp. 231–46.

Miller, V. J. (2006) 'Contexts: Theology, Devotion, and Culture', in T. K. Beal and T. Linafelt (eds) *Mel Gibson's Bible*, Chicago, IL: University of Chicago.

Mueller, D. A. (1993) *Eyes upon the Cross: A Cycle of Plays for Lent*, Boston, MA: Baker's Plays.

Munoz, L. (2004) 'Does R Rating Really Tell the Story of "Passion"?', *Los Angeles Times*, 2 February. Available from: http://articles.latimes.com/2004/feb/02/entertainment/ et-munoz2 (accessed December 2008).

Murdock, G. (1997) 'Reservoirs of Dogma: An Archaeology of Popular Anxieties', in M. Barker and J. Petley (eds) *Ill Effects: The Media/Violence Debate*, London and New York: Routledge.

Musser, C. (1996) 'Passions and the Passion Play: Theater, Film, and Religion in America, 1880–1900', in F. G. Couvares (ed.) *Movie Censorship and American Culture*, Washington, DC: Smithsonian Institution.

Neff, D. (2004) 'The Passion of Mel Gibson', *Christianity Today* vol. 48 no. 3, pp. 30–5.

New Zealand Press Association (2004a) 'Plea on R16 "Passion" Rating', *New Zealand Herald*, Life & Style, 23 February. Available from: http://www.nzherald.co.nz/lifestyle/news/ article.cfm?c_id=6&objectid=3550727 (accessed November 2008).

New Zealand Press Association (2004b) 'NZ Churches Join Push to Lower Censorship of the Passion', *New Zealand Herald*, Life & Style, 24 February. Available from: http://www.nzherald.co.nz/nz/news/article.cfm?c_id=1&objectid=3551015 (accessed November 2008).

Noll, M. A. (2002) 'Evangelicals, Past and Present', in E. W. Blumhofer (ed.) *Religion, Politics, and the American Experience: Reflections on Religion and American Public Life*, Tuscaloosa: University of Alabama Press.

Noxon, C. (2003) 'Is the Pope Catholic … Enough?', *New York Times Magazine*, 9 March, pp. 50–3, SM.

O'Reilly, B. (Moderator) (2003) 'Personal Story: Mel Gibson', *The O'Reilly Factor*, Fox News, broadcast 17 January.

Overstreet, J. (2004) 'Film Forum: Excruciating? Excellent? Reviews of *The Passion of The Christ*', *Christianity Today*, 26 February. Available from: http://www.christianitytoday.com/ ct/2004/februaryweb-only/040226.html (accessed December 2008).

Peterson, T. (2004) 'Mixed Global Reception for "Passion"', *People.com*. Available from: http://www.people.com/people/article/0,,628030,00.html (accessed 5 March 2004).

Petrakis, J. (2004) 'Tough Guy', *Christian Century* vol. 121 no. 6, p. 40.

Potter, W. J. (2003) *The 11 Myths of Media Violence*, Thousand Oaks, CA: Sage Publications.

Prince, S. (1998) *Savage Cinema: Sam Peckinpah and the Rise of Ultraviolent Movies*, Austin: University of Texas Press.

Prince, S. (2003) *Classical Film Violence: Designing and Regulating Brutality in Hollywood Cinema, 1930–1968*, New Brunswick, NJ: Rutgers University Press.

Prince, S. (2006) 'Beholding Blood Sacrifice in *The Passion of the Christ*: How Real Is Movie Violence?', *Film Quarterly* vol. 59 no. 4, pp. 11–22.

Regnerus, M. D. and Smith, C. (1998) 'Selective Deprivatization among American Religious Traditions: The Reversal of the Great Reversal', *Social Forces* vol. 76 no. 4, pp. 1347–72.

Reinhartz, A. (2002) 'The Gospel of John: How 'the Jews' Became Part of the Plot', in P. Fredriksen and A. Reinhartz (eds) *Jesus, Judaism, and Christian Anti-Judaism: Reading the New Testament after the Holocaust*, Louisville, KY: Westminster John Knox Press.

Rich, F. (2003) 'Mel Gibson's Martyrdom Complex', *New York Times*, 3 August, Arts, pp. 1, 4.

Rolfe, D. (2004) 'Hollywood Looks for the Next "Passion"'. Available from: http://www.dove.org/fyi/articles/thenextpassion.htm (accessed 22 March 2005).

Rooney, D. (2002) 'Mel Driven by "Passion"', *Daily Variety* vol. 276 no. 79, pp. 1, 26.

Rubenstein, R. L. (2006) 'Mel Gibson's Passion', in T. K. Beal and T. Linafelt (eds) *Mel Gibson's Bible*, Chicago, IL: University of Chicago Press.

Sandler, K. S. (2007) *The Naked Truth: Why Hollywood Doesn't Make X-Rated Movies*, New Brunswick, NJ: Rutgers University Press.

Sawyer, D. (Moderator) (2004) 'Mel Gibson's Passion: An Interview with Mel Gibson', *ABC Primetime*, ABC News, broadcast 16 February.

Sawyer, D. (Moderator) (2006) 'Mel Gibson Interview', *Good Morning America*, ABC News, broadcast 13 October.

SBBFC (2009) *The Passion of the Christ*. Available from: http://www.sbbfc.co.uk/ CaseStudies/Passion_of_the_Christ (accessed 5 March 2009).

Schmöger, C. E. (1976) *The Life and Times of Anne Catherine Emmerich* (vol. I), Rockrod, IL: Tan Books.

Segal, A. F. (2004) 'How I Stopped Worrying about Mel Gibson and Learned to Love the Quest for the Historical Jesus: A Review of Mel Gibson's *The Passion of the Christ*', *Journal for the Study of the Historical Jesus* vol. 2 no. 2, pp. 190–208.

Shepherd, D., Fitzgerald, B., Fulco, W., Bach, A. and Jefford, C. N. (2004) *From Gospel to Gibson: An Interview with the Writers*, paper presented at the 2004 Annual Meeting of the Society of Biblical Literature, 21 November, San Antonio, TX.

Shibley, M. A. (1996) *Resurgent Evangelicalism in the United States: Mapping Cultural Change since 1970*, Columbia: University of South Carolina Press.

Silk, M. (2004) 'Gibson's Passion: A Case Study in Media Manipulation?', *Journal of Religion & Society* (Supplement Series 1), pp. 1–7.

Slocum, J. D. (2005) 'Cinema and the Civilizing Process: Rethinking Violence in the World War II Combat Film', *Cinema Journal* vol. 44 no. 3, pp. 35–63.

Smith, C. (2003) *The Secular Revolution: Power, Interests, and Conflict in the Secularization of American Public Life*, Berkeley: University of California Press.

Smith, C. and Emerson, M. (1998) *American Evangelicalism: Embattled and Thriving*, Chicago, IL: University of Chicago Press.

Smith, S. (2003) 'Who'll Buy Mel's Movie?', *Newsweek* vol. 142 no. 15, p. 72.

Smithouser, B., Isaac, S. and Neven, T. (2004) *The Passion of the Christ*, *Plugged In*, 24 February. Available from: http://www.pluggedin.com/videos/2005/q1/ passionofthechrist.aspx (accessed 22 March, 2009).

Sobran, J. (2004) 'Gibson and His Psyche', 24 February. Available from: http://sobran.com/ columns/2004/040224.shtml (accessed 12 March 2009).

SPCS (2004a) 'SPCS Appeals Passion of Christ R16 Classification', press release, 2008.

SPCS (2004b) 'Response to Chief Censor Bill Hastings', press release, 2008.

SPCS (2004c) 'Chief Censor Misuses Living Word', press release, 2008.

SPCS (2005) 'Chief Censor's Misuse of Living Word'. Available from: http://www.spcs.org.nz/2005/chief-censors-misuse-of-living-word/ (accessed December 2008).

Spencer, M. (2009) 'The Coming Evangelical Collapse', *Christian Science Monitor* vol. 101 no. 71, p. 9.

Springhall, J. (1998) *Youth, Popular Culture and Moral Panics: Penny Gaffs to Gangsta-Rap, 1830–1996*, New York: St Martin's Press.

Starker, S. (1989) *Evil Influences: Crusades against the Mass Media*, New Brunswick, NJ: Transaction Publishers.

Sterritt, D. (2004) 'Gibson's "Passion" Has Little but Suffering on Its Mind', 25 February. Available from: http://www.csmonitor.com/2004/0225/p13s01-almo.html (accessed 12 March 2004).

Stossel, S. (1997) 'The Man Who Counts the Killings', *Atlantic Monthly* vol. 279 no. 5, pp. 86–104.

Straughn, J. B. and Feld, S. L. (2010) 'America as a "Christian Nation"? Understanding Religious Boundaries of National Identity in the United States', *Sociology of Religion* vol. 71 no. 3, pp. 280–306.

Sumner, J. (2004) 'Gibson Set Stage for "Passion" with Controlled Marketing: The Greatest Story Ever Sold?', *Dallas Morning News*, 17 February. Available from: http://www.alarryross.com/inthenews/greatestStoryEverSold.htm (accessed November 2008).

Szalai, G. (2005) 'Regal Settles Icon's Lawsuit over "Passion"', *Billboard Law Newsletter*, 8 March.

Thistlethwaite, S. B. (2004) 'Mel Makes a War Movie', in J. Burnham (ed.) *Perspectives on The Passion of the Christ: Religious Thinkers and Writers Explore the Issues Raised by the Controversial Movie*, New York: Hyperion.

Thistlethwaite, S. B. (2009) 'Why the Faithful Approve of Torture', *Washington Post*, 1 May. Available from: http://newsweek.washingtonpost.com/onfaith/panelists/susan_brooks_thistlethwaite/2009/05/why_the_faithful_approve_of_torture.html?hpid=talkbox1 (accessed May 2009).

Thompson, K. (1999) *Storytelling in the New Hollywood: Understanding Classical Narrative Technique*, Cambridge, MA: Harvard University Press.

TMZ (2006) 'Gibson's Anti-Semitic Tirade – Alleged Cover Up', *TMZ*, 28 July. Available from: http://www.tmz.com/2006/07/28/gibsons-anti-semitic-tirade-alleged-cover-up/ (accessed 16 February 2009).

Walsh, F. (1996) *Sin and Censorship: The Catholic Church and the Motion Picture Industry*, New Haven, CT: Yale University Press.

Walsh, R. G. (2008) '*The Passion* as Horror Film: St. Mel of the Cross', *Journal of Religion and Popular Culture* vol. XX. Available from: http://www.usask.ca/relst/jrpc/art20-passionashorror.html (accessed February 2009).

Warren, H. (2001) 'Southern Baptists as Audience and Public: A Cultural Analysis of the Disney Boycott', in D. A. Stout and J. M. Buddenbaum (eds) *Religion and Popular Culture: Studies on the Interaction of Worldviews*, Ames: Iowa State University Press.

Wattenberg, B. (Moderator) (1995) 'Does Hollywood Hurt America?', *Think Tank with Ben Wattenberg*, Public Broadcasting Service, broadcast 16 June.

Watts, R. (2004) 'A Matter of Horizons, *The Passion* through the Looking Glass: A Response to Alan F. Segal's Review', *Journal for the Study of the Historical Jesus* vol. 2 no. 2, pp. 224–9.

Wieseltier, L. (2004) 'The Worship of Blood', *New Republic* vol. 230 no. 8, pp. 19–21.

Wilmington, M. (2004) Movie Review: 'The Passion of the Christ'. Available from: http://chicago.metromix.com/movies/review/movie-review-the-passion/158690/content (accessed 5 March 2004).

Winn, P. (2000) 'Irrefutable Link', *CitizenLink: A Website of Focus on the Family*, 21 August. Available from: http://www.family.org/cforum/feature/a0012613.cfm (accessed March 2002).

Witherington III, B. (2004) 'Numbstruck: An Evangelical Reflects on Mel Gibson's *Passion*', in J. Burnham (ed.) *Perspectives on The Passion of the Christ: Religious Thinkers and Writers Explore the Issues Raised by the Controversial Movie*, New York: Hyperion.

Women Influencing the Nation (2004) Petition, April. Available from: http://www.seethepassion.com/petition.php (accessed 5 March 2004).

Zeitchik, S. (2006) 'Religious Experience', *Variety* vol. 404 no. 11, p. 14.

Zenit (2003a) 'Mel Gibson's Great Passion', 6 March. Available from: http://www.zenit.org/ article-6722?l=english (accessed 22 March 2009).

Zenit (2003b) 'Controversy Swirls around Mel Gibson's "Passion"', 30 May. Available from: http://www.zenit.org/article-7391?l=english (accessed 5 March 2009).

Index